Anonymous

Directory and Ceremonial of the Office for the Religious

Of Our Lady of Charity of the Good Shepherd of Angers

Anonymous

Directory and Ceremonial of the Office for the Religious
Of Our Lady of Charity of the Good Shepherd of Angers

ISBN/EAN: 9783744653602

Printed in Europe, USA, Canada, Australia, Japan

Cover: Foto ©Lupo / pixelio.de

More available books at **www.hansebooks.com**

DIRECTORY
AND
CEREMONIAL OF THE OFFICE.

ROEHAMPTON:
PRINTED BY JOHN GRIFFIN.

Live Jesus and Mary!

DIRECTORY

AND

CEREMONIAL OF THE OFFICE

FOR THE RELIGIOUS

OF

Our Lady of Charity of the Good Shepherd of Angers.

ORDER OF ST. AUGUSTINE.

CONFORMABLE TO THE ROMAN RITE.

———

1899.

This Directory and Ceremonial have been drawn up with great care, and are calculated to promote the devotion of the Religious and the exact observance of their Constitutions. We recommend their use, desiring that they should be faithfully observed in all the houses of the Institute of the Good Shepherd of Angers.

Rome, November 21st, 1897.

✠ C. Card. Mazzella,
Bishop of Palestrina, Protector.

NOTICE.

THE Divine Office is a vocal and public prayer, composed of all that is most remarkable and instructive in the Books of Holy Scripture, in the writings of the Fathers of the Church, and in the Lives of the Saints. The Church orders that it should be recited at certain hours of the day and night, in the name of the whole body of the faithful, by those who are specially set apart for this duty. 1. To give to God the honour which is due to Him. 2. To thank Him for all the benefits we continually receive from His infinite goodness. 3. To very humbly ask pardon for our sins. 4. To implore His divine assistance and His infinite mercy.

The better to understand this definition, it must be remarked that there are two kinds of prayer, one public, the other private; private prayer is that which the faithful make according to their devotion, when they pray mentally or vocally, saying the prayers that their particular devotion inspires; public prayer is that which is made for and in the name of the Church, by those who are required by their state to recite the Divine Office in the words she has expressly ordained; and thus in whatever manner Religious in the Orders established by the Church, recite their Breviary or Office, whether in public or private, their prayer is always public, because it is ordered by the Church, and made in her name. On the contrary, if a layman through devotion recite the canonical hours, his prayer is not public, but private, although said in the Church, because he is not deputed by the Church, as are all those who are bound by their holy vocation to this sacred duty.[1]

It must, however, be acknowledged that, to acquit themselves worthily of this holy obligation, Religious must not be satisfied with interior worship (although this is the most essential, as our Lord said to the Samaritan woman), but they must join to it the exterior; they must show respect for the Divine Majesty by the decorum and gravity of their outward demeanour, attending exactly to the ceremonies which the Church, inspired by the Holy Spirit, has so holily prescribed.

This it is which has induced the Religious of Our Lady of Charity of the Good Shepherd of Angers to draw up this Directory and Ceremonial, in order that there may be uniformity in all the houses of the Institute, and that everywhere the Divine worship may be carried out with the devotion that so sacred a duty requires.

The Religious of Our Lady of Charity cannot fail to be greatly attached to the Office, if they reflect how ardently their Venerable Founder desired that they should acquit themselves of it well and faithfully.

He zealously recommended it to the first Mothers of the Congregation, as one of the duties essential for the glory of God and their own sanctification; he taught this by word as well as by example, since it is related in his life that the moment he heard the bell ring for the Office, he left everything to go to it; the bell being for him the command of the great King, which did not permit the delay of a single instant.

It is then to be hoped that having followed in this

---

[1] Cf. Suarez, *De Statu Religionis*, Tract iv. L. iv. chap. ix. pp. 7, 8.

Directory and Ceremonial, as exactly as possible, the Rubrics of the Missal, of the Breviary, and Roman Ritual, all the Religious of Our Lady of Charity of the Good Shepherd of Angers, as true daughters of the Church, will gladly accept them, and prove for themselves that the order, the uniformity, and the majesty of these exterior ceremonies aid not a little to recollection, attention, and interior devotion. This is the fruit which is hoped for from the pains that have been taken in this work, and in explaining briefly and clearly matters which in themselves are rather difficult.

Andegaven.	Translation.
Quum in singulis Ecclesiis vel Oratoriis adnexis Domibus Monialium a Caritate Boni Pastoris nuncupatarum, quotannis die octava Februarii solemnitas in honorem Purissimi Cordis Beatæ Mariæ Virginis institui soleat, hodierna ipsarum Monalium Superiorissa in Andegavensi Primaria Domo residens, Sanctissimum Dominum Nostrum Leonem Papam XIII. humillimis precibus rogavit ut Missa votiva solemnis de eodem Purissimo Corde cum *Gloria* et *Credo* enuntiata die in præfatis Ecclesiis vel Oratoriis cantari valeat. Sanctitas porro Sua, referente subscripto Sacrorum Rituum Congregationis Secretario, attento præsertim commendationis Officio Rmi. Ordinarii Diœceseos Andegavensis, benigne annuere dignata est pro gratia petita Missæ solemnis; dummodo non occurrat Duplex primæ	Whereas in the Churches and Oratories attached to each of the Convents of the Sisters of Our Lady of Charity of the Good Shepherd, it is customary to observe on the eighth day of February in each year, a Solemn Feast in honour of the Most Pure Heart of Mary, the present Superior of the said Sisters, residing in the Mother House at Angers, has most humbly petitioned Our Holy Father Pope Leo XIII. that on that day a Solemn Votive Mass of the Most Pure Heart of Mary, with *Gloria* and *Credo*, may be sung in all the aforesaid Churches and Oratories. Wherefore, His Holiness, on the report of the undersigned Secretary of the Sacred Congregation of Rites, and on the special recommendation of his Lordship the Bishop of Angers, has graciously granted permission for this

classis, vel Dominica prima Quadragesimæ, aut aliquod Festum Deiparæ, nec non Feria IV. Cinerum: servatis Rubricis Contrariis non obstantibus quibuscumque.

Die 27 Januarii, 1892.

Solemn Mass; provided that no Double of the First Class, nor First Sunday of Lent, nor any Feast of the Blessed Virgin, nor Ash Wednesday, falls on that day. Granted, subject to the due observance of the Rubrics, all other things to the contrary notwithstanding.

The 27th day of January, 1892.

✠ CAJ. CARDINALIS
    ALOISI MASELLA, *Præf.*

✠ CAJETAN CARD.
    ALOYSIUS MASELLA, *Pref.*

VINC. NUSSI, *Secret.*

VINC. NUSSI, *Secret.*

LIVE JESUS AND MARY!

Directory of the Choir,

WITH EXPLANATION OF

The Ceremonies of the Divine Office,

FOR THE RELIGIOUS OF OUR LADY OF CHARITY OF THE GOOD SHEPHERD OF ANGERS.

OF THE OFFICE IN GENERAL.

The Religious of Our Lady of Charity of the Good Shepherd will ordinarily say the little Office of the most Blessed Virgin, as reformed by the holy Council of Trent and Pope Urban VIII.

This little Office of the Blessed Virgin takes the place for them, of the Divine Office; they recite it in the name of the Church and in union with her, honouring also, by the commemorations, the Mysteries and the Saints, of which the Church celebrates the feast.

To show more clearly this intimate union with the liturgy of the Church, Religious Communities ought, when reciting the Office in public, to conform to the Rules of the Roman Breviary, as to the Seasons and Feasts, doubling the antiphons when the Church celebrates a feast which is double (S.C.R., July 11th, 1866), reciting the *Te Deum*, or omitting it according as it is recited or not in the Divine Office, etc.

PARTICULAR OBSERVATIONS.

1. The antiphons should always be doubled when the feast ranks as a double. The last day of an octave is always double, but no extra ceremonies should be added.

2. The *Te Deum* is said throughout the year. During Advent and from Septuagesima to Easter, it is omitted on Sundays, and on days when there is no commemoration, or only that of a simple. It is also said during all the octaves that occur at these times.

3. All Sundays (except *Low Sunday*, which is a double) are semi-doubles; the first Sundays of Advent and Lent, Passion and Palm Sundays, being privileged Sundays of the first class, take precedence at Lauds of all other commemorations; the second, third, and fourth Sundays of Advent and Lent, Septuagesima, Sexagesima, and Quinquagesima, being privileged Sundays of the second class, take precedence at Lauds of all feasts that are not first class.

The first Vespers—that is to say, the Vespers of Saturday, as well as those of the second Vespers of Sunday, take precedence of semi-doubles; they even take precedence of minor doubles if these fall on the same day, for in this case the Church says the Office of the Sunday, and a commemoration only is made of these minor doubles, according to the decision of the Sacred Congregation of Rites. The commemorations of Doctors are an exception, they must be transferred to the day fixed by the Ordo. The antiphons are not doubled, and the *Sancti Dei omnes* or the *Ecce Dominus veniet* are said at Lauds, as well as at the first and second Vespers. The same rule is to be followed for Vigils and privileged ferias.

4. If two commemorations occur, of which the anthems and versicles are the same, for example, two Confessors not Bishops, for the second commemoration, the anthem and versicle of Lauds are taken for the first Vespers, and at Lauds, the anthem and versicle of the first Vespers. The antiphons, versicles, and prayers of the commemoration are changed when they are the same as in the ordinary Office; this occurs especially on some feasts of the Blessed Virgin; for example, the second Sunday in October, feast of the Maternity of the Blessed Virgin, when the prayer is *Deus qui de Beatæ Mariæ Virginis*, which is the same as that of the ordinary Office at Lauds. Then the prayer *Concede*

nos famulos tuos is taken from the common for feasts of the Blessed Virgin. The versicle *Lætamini*, which is said after the *Sancti Dei* in the ordinary Office, being also the common for Martyrs, ought to be replaced in the commemoration by *Exultabunt Sancti in gloria.*

On the feasts of Martyrs, when a third V. and R. are needed, the V. and R. for the 4th of November, "*Exultent justi in conspectu Dei.*" R. "*Et delectentur in lætitia*" are taken. For a Confessor, as on the 14th January, "*Elegit eum Dominus Sacerdotem sibi.*" R. "*Ad sacrificandum hostiam laudis.*" For a Virgin, 22nd July, "*Elegit eam Deus et pre-elegit eam.*" R. "*In tabernaculo suo habitare facit eam.*"

5. Whenever a psalm is sung, the corresponding antiphon ought also to be sung; the same at the *Magnificat*, *Nunc Dimittis*, and *Benedictus*.

Calendar of Fixed Feasts
ACCORDING TO THE MONTHS.

JANUARY.

1st. THE CIRCUMCISION.—On the eve of this feast, the Obedience is rung a little before eight o clock, and after it the Sisters go to the choir to make the act of reparation. On the day of the feast, after the mid-day obedience, the prayer in the Spiritual Exercises for the first of January is said. This practice is, however, observed without obligation.

The Office of the Dead ought not to be said during this quarantine unless at the decease of a Religious in the house.

6th. THE EPIPHANY.—This is a solemn Feast of the first class, with an octave. At the Mass of the day and during the octave, the Sisters genuflect when the Priest says the words of the Gospel, *Procedentes adoraverunt eum.* Each day of the octave has a proper antiphon at the *Magnificat* and *Benedictus*, these days must be counted exclusive of the Sunday. For example: if the Sunday falls on the third day of the octave, on the Monday will be made the commemoration of the third day, the following day, the fourth, and so on.

The second Sunday after the Epiphany, FEAST OF THE HOLY NAME OF JESUS, Mass is sung. If Septuagesima falls on that day, the feast of the Holy Name is transferred to the 28th of January.

20th. SAINT FABIAN and SAINT SEBASTIAN.—The Sisters go in procession to the Infirmary; the Litany of Our

Lady may be sung going and returning. In the Infirmary, before the altar, the hymn of the Martyrs is sung; the Sister who officiates says the versicle and prayer of the feast.

29th. SAINT FRANCIS DE SALES.—Holiday of Rule. The Institute having special obligation to honour this Saint, the Assistant officiates, and there is a sermon, if possible. In the Convent at Angers, the first Vespers and the *Te Deum* have always been sung. Mantles are worn. The *Preface* to the Rule of Saint Augustine is read in the Refectory during dinner.

FEBRUARY.

2nd. THE PURIFICATION.—Terce, Sext, and None are said at a quarter to eight. Immediately after, the candles are blessed, during which the Sisters stand turned to the altar, and in choir while they are distributed. The same is observed for the Ashes and Palms. At the first prayer of the blessing of the candles, the convent bell is rung to give notice to the absent.

When the celebrant receives his candle from the deacon, the Sister Sacristan makes a sign to the chanters to begin. They immediately intone *Lumen ad revelationem gentium*, which the choir continues. The versicle being finished, the chanters commence the *Nunc dimittis*, and after each verse the choir repeats *Lumen*, &c., until the distribution is finished, leaving the *Gloria Patri* for the end.

At the last prayer of the blessing of the candles, which begins *Domine Jesu Christe, qui hodierna die*, the Superior and the Assistant go to the grate to receive their candles; the Sisters follow in their rank, two and two, having their veils down. They genuflect to the Blessed Sacrament as usual. They kneel to receive the candle and kiss it in the Priest's hand. Towards the end of the ceremony, the chanters intone the antiphon *Exsurge*, which the choir continues. They sing the psalm *Deus auribus* and the *Gloria Patri* to the mediant; the choir having finished it, the chanters repeat the antiphon *Exsurge*, at the end of which the Sisters turn towards the altar, bending the right knee when *Flectamus genua* is said after *Septuagesima*.

When the Priest begins the prayer, *Exaudi quæsumus*, which is said after the distribution of the candles, the Sisters who are to carry the cross and candles, place themselves in the middle of the choir, in order that after the deacon has sung *Procedamus in pace*, and that he has been answered *In nomine Christi, Amen*, they may immediately commence the procession. All follow in good order, holding their candles to the inside of the procession—that is, the Sisters of one choir holding them in the right hand, the other choir in the left. The bell for the procession serves for the first bell for Mass, and therefore they toll ten or twelve strokes at the end.

Beginning the procession, the chanters intone the anthems *Adorna thalamum* and *Accepit Simeon*, as they are in the Gradual. They do not stop as they pass before the Altar in the cloister. On returning, when the cross-bearer enters the Church, the chanters commence the response *Obtulerunt pro eo*, which the choir continues as it is in the Gradual. The response being finished, those who carry the cross and candlesticks, put them back in their places and take their candles again. After the bell has been rung at the return of the procession, the last bell for Mass is tolled. The Sisters hold their candles lighted during the Gospel, and from the Canon till the Communion inclusively; after which they may lay them down.

8th. SOLEMNITY OF THE MOST HOLY HEART OF MARY.—This is the Titular feast of the Congregation, and of first rank. The first Vespers, which are proper to this feast, are sung. During the three days of retreat, the extra meditations are made on the subject of the feast, as also that of the evening during the octave. On this day the *Wishes* of our Venerable Father Eudes are read in the Refectory during dinner.

The Sisters communicate with the intention of gaining

the Plenary Indulgence granted to Religious persons on the principal feast of their Order, according to the extract from the Bull of Paul V.

The Blessed Sacrament is exposed from the first Vespers.

Remark.—For all the Expositions and Benedictions mentioned in the course of this book, permission must, in the first place, be asked of the Ordinary.

At Compline (which they advance a quarter of an hour), the Superior standing in her stall, and the choir turned towards the Altar, the first chorist goes above the lectern to ask the blessing for the short lesson, saying *Jube*, &c.; she inclines, turning a little towards the Superior, and when she says *Tu autem*, she genuflects and retires; the choir answers *Deo gratias;* the Superior says *Adjutorium nostrum*, &c., the Sisters answer *Qui fecit cœlum*, &c.; then the *Pater* is said in secret. The Superior, inclining profoundly, begins the *Confiteor* in a lower tone, saying *Et vobis fratres*, and at the end *Et vos fratres*. The Sisters turn in choir when she begins; they do not answer *Amen* at the end, but say immediately *Misereatur tui*, &c.; the Superior answers *Amen* as she rises, and the Sisters inclining, begin the *Confiteor*, turning a little towards her as they say *Et tibi Pater*, and *Et te Pater*. The Superior says *Misereatur vestri* and *Indulgentiam*, making the sign of the Cross on herself, and the choir do the same, answering *Amen* as they rise. The Superior, in her stall, says, in a higher tone, *Converte nos*, &c., and *Deus in adjutorium*, &c. After the *Gloria Patri*, the first chorist intones the antiphon *Miserere*, and the chanter the first psalm, *Cum invocarem*. The Superior intones the antiphon, *Salva nos*, and the first chanter the *Nunc Dimittis*. When Compline of the Divine Office is said in private, the *Confiteor* is said only once, and the *Misereatur* and *Indulgentiam* in the plural.

The evening Obedience is rung at half-past seven.—*Pater*, *Ave*, and *Credo* are said in secret at the commencement of Matins and Prime of the Divine Office, before the other hours only a *Pater* and *Ave*.—At the mid-day Obedience the Assistant names two Sisters of each choir to say the first four lessons.

At the end of the hymn of Matins, the first chorist intones the first antiphon, and the chanter the first psalm. She who is to say the first lesson, goes to the middle of the choir when the Superior says *Et ne nos* of the *Pater;* she makes a genuflexion, and after the *Amen* at the end of the absolution, she turns a little towards the Superior to ask the blessing; having received it she rises and commences the lesson, inclining profoundly when she says *Tu autem,* &c.; she waits to say the versicle with the Sister named to say the second lesson, who goes out at the beginning of the response to join the other Sister in the middle of the choir; having said the versicle together, they genuflect, she who has said the lesson retires while the other Sister asks the blessing. The Sister who is to say the third lesson goes out at the beginning of the response, which precedes the lesson she has to say, observing the same ceremonies; the Sister who has said the second lesson returns at the third response, to assist her to say the versicle and the *Gloria Patri*, at the end of which they genuflect together and retire.

The second nocturn falls to the Assistant's choir, who intones the first psalm after the second chorist has begun the first antiphon. Those who are to say the lessons observe the ceremonies marked for the first nocturn, but the two last lessons are always said by the chorists.

The third nocturn returns to the Superior's choir; the chanters say the first two lessons, the Superior says the last, with the same ceremonies as at the ordinary Office. The choir remains standing during the text of the Holy Gospel; after the words *Et reliqua*, she who says them makes a pause, all sit down, and she continues the homily.

On the day of the feast the Blessed Sacrament is exposed after Mass. The servants and "*classes*" keep this feast.

When the chapter at Prime is commenced, the Sisters turn towards the altar as usual; they incline at the *Gloria Patri* without turning round. They do not make the sign of the Cross at the *Deus in adjutorium*, which is said three times. The Superior says the *Kyrie*, which the choir answers. The first chorist goes out to say the short lesson when the prayer *Dirigere* is being said, with the ceremonies observed at Compline. The short responsaries at the four Little Hours and at Compline are said by the two chorists, who go out at the beginning of the chapter as usual. All the psalms of the Hours are begun by the first chanter, except the two last of Prime, which the Assistant or second chanter intones.

After None, which is said before Mass, the Celebrant with his Ministers, kneeling before the Altar, intones the *Veni Creator*, which the Religious continue alternately; or else the Priests form one choir and they the other.

The Celebrant says the versicle and prayer, at the end of which the chanters begin the Introit very solemnly. After Mass the Celebrant intones the *Te Deum*, which is continued alternately; he says the versicle *Benedicamus Patrem*, &c., and the prayers *Omnipotens sempiterne* and *Deus cujus misericordia*, in thanksgiving that on this day, in the year 1651, this Congregation was established. At the end of the *Te Deum*, the Kiss of Peace is given. For the Mass, see the Decree, page 11.

OF THE OCTAVE.

Every day during the octave, the Blessed Sacrament is exposed before Vespers, which are sung; Compline is rung at half-past four, at which the *Nunc Dimittis* is sung. Benediction follows.

When the feast of the Heart of Mary occurs in Lent, the feast only is kept, omitting the octave. If Ash Wednesday falls during the octave, it is terminated the preceding Tuesday without doubling the antiphons or taking the first Vespers. In this case Benediction of the Blessed Sacrament is not given.

MARCH.

19th. FEAST OF SAINT JOSEPH, double of the first class, holiday of Rule. Our Congregation ought to have a particular devotion to this Saint, and celebrate his feast solemnly.

The first and second Vespers are sung, the *Nunc Dimittis* at Compline, the *Te Deum* and *Benedictus* at Matins. There should be a sermon, if possible. If there is a procession to the Oratory of the Saint, the hymn *Te Joseph Celebrent* or *Cœlitum Joseph* is sung. The *Stabat* is not sung either on the eve or day of the feast.

When the feast of Saint Joseph falls in Holy Week, it is transferred till after the octave of Easter, to the day fixed by the Church; it is kept with the same solemnity as the day of the feast.

25th. ANNUNCIATION OF THE BLESSED VIRGIN, double of the first class. The Office of Advent is taken, beginning at the first Vespers, and the final anthem, *Ave Regina Cœlorum* is said.

On the eve and on the day of the feast the versicle *Angelus Domini*, &c., is said at the end of the Litany of the Blessed Virgin. The *Stabat* is not sung either on the eve or day of the feast.

The bell for Vespers is rung at half a quarter past ten on both days. Terce at eight. If the feast falls during Holy Week or Easter Week the Office is transferred to Monday in Low Week, and begins at the first Vespers. In this case all is as solemn as on the day of the feast, with the *Alleluias* in their place.

APRIL.

24th. ANNIVERSARY OF THE PRECIOUS DEATH OF OUR VENERABLE MOTHER FOUNDRESS. The intention of the Holy Communion will be to thank God for the graces granted to her and to the whole Institute.

25th. SAINT MARK, EVANGELIST. The procession takes place either immediately before or after Mass, and the four Little Hours are said at eight o'clock. When the procession is after Mass, the Convent bell is rung before Communion, to give notice to the absent Sisters. During the last Gospel the two chanters kneel in the middle of the choir, and when it is finished they intone the anthem *Exsurge Domine*. Those who carry the cross and candlesticks stand before the altar, as usual, whilst the choir continues the antiphon. The chanters say the psalm and the *Gloria Patri*, and repeat the antiphon, as at the Introit (which is likewise observed whenever the Greater Litanies are sung in procession): they begin the Litany of the Saints, which they double as far as *Sancta Maria*, after which the procession starts; it is made in the garden if possible. The prayers, &c., are said, as they are in the Roman Gradual. If the weather does not allow the Sisters to go into the garden, they take two or three turns in the cloister, to finish the Litany. They sing twice *Sancte Marce*, and contrive to sing the *Agnus Dei* as they re-enter the choir. The Sister who officiates, kneeling in the middle of the choir, intones the *Pater Noster*, says the rest in secret, till *Et ne nos inducas*, which she says in psalmody; the choir answers *Sed libera nos a malo;* the chanters kneeling behind the Sister who officiates, commence the psalm *Deus in adjutorium*, which they say alternately with the choir. After the *Gloria Patri* the Sister who officiates takes up the versicle, *Salvos fac servos tuos*, and those that follow, to which the choir answers. At the versicle *Domine exaudi orationem meam*, she rises, says the prayers which follow the Litany, ending with the versicle *Fidelium*. The chanters remain kneeling until the end of the prayers, when they retire.

The Religious of the choir who have not been able to assist at the procession should say the Litany of the Saints in private.

JUNE.

29th. SAINT PETER AND SAINT PAUL. In Convents where the Community is large enough, the Office proper to the feast may be said. During the octave the prayer *Protege* is omitted at Vespers and Lauds, taking only *Omnes Sancti tui*, and this should be observed every time commemoration is made of Saint Peter and Saint Paul.

JULY.

2nd. VISITATION OF THE BLESSED VIRGIN, holiday of rule. The *Nunc Dimittis* is sung at Compline, and the *Te Deum* at Matins.

The procession is made to the Novitiate; going and returning the Litany of the Blessed Virgin is sung, and the *Magnificat* before the Altar.

22nd. FEAST OF SAINT MARY MAGDALEN. There is a procession made to the Magdalens and Penitents. Going and returning the hymns of the Saint are sung, and some antiphon or response before her Altar.

31st. FEAST OF SAINT IGNATIUS. On this day our Convent at Angers was founded in 1829, under the title of the *Good Shepherd*, to perpetuate the remembrance of an ancient house of this name, where girls and women were received for penance and preservation.

The intention of the Holy Communion will be in thanksgiving for the foundation of our Congregation.

AUGUST.

2nd. Plenary Indulgence for the Portiuncula.

15th. THE ASSUMPTION OF THE MOST BLESSED VIRGIN, double of the first class with octave. The Blessed Sacrament is exposed.

19th. ANNIVERSARY OF THE PRECIOUS DEATH OF THE VENERABLE FATHER JOHN EUDES, Missionary Priest of the Congregation of Jesus and Mary, our Founder. The intention of the Holy Communion will be to thank God for the graces granted to him and to us by his intercession.

21st. FEAST OF SAINT JANE FRANCES DE CHANTAL. The intention of the Holy Communion will be to obtain the Religious spirit which she possessed so perfectly.

28th. FEAST OF SAINT AUGUSTINE, our Blessed Legislator, holiday of Rule, double of the first class with octave. There is Exposition of the Blessed Sacrament. Plenary Indulgence is granted to all Religious who combat under his rule. There is a sermon, if possible. At dinner the *Preface* to our holy Rule by Saint Francis de Sales is read.

SEPTEMBER.

The Sunday in the octave of the Nativity of the Blessed Virgin, the FEAST OF THE HOLY NAME OF MARY is celebrated, and no commemoration of the octave is made.

14th. FEAST OF THE EXALTATION OF THE HOLY CROSS. If this feast falls on the Sunday within the octave of the Nativity, the feast of the Name of Mary is transferred to the day fixed in the *Ordo;* but when the feast of the Nativity falls on a Saturday, the Name of Mary is kept on the Sunday, omitting the first Vespers. If the octave day of the Nativity occurs on this same Sunday, commemoration of the Name of Mary is made, omitting that of the octave day.

NOVEMBER.

1st. FEAST OF ALL SAINTS, double of the first class, with octave. The *Sancti Dei omnes* is omitted during the whole octave. At the end of the prayer of the first Vespers, the bell is tolled five times, to give notice to the Sisters to come and draw the Beatitudes. The Superior says first, the *Veni Sancte*, or the anthem *Angeli, Archangeli,* &c.

The Litany of the Saints is said every day during the octave after Compline; all is omitted which follows the *Omnes Sancti et Sanctæ Dei*, &c., the three *Agnus Dei* are said, then the anthem *Sancti Dei omnes*, the versicle *Lætamini in Domino*, and the prayers *Omnes Sancti*, finishing by the short termination, "*Per Christum Dominum nostrum*," which is used whenever prayers are said at other times than the Office, or else by the termination, "*Qui vivis et regnas*," &c., according as the prayers are addressed to the Eternal Father or to God the Son.

2nd. COMMEMORATION OF THE FAITHFUL DEPARTED. After the *Benedicamus Domino* of the second Vespers of All Saints, Vespers of the Dead are commenced. The Superior intones the antiphon *Placebo Domino*, which is doubled; the chanter the psalm *Dilexi*, and the others consecutively, observing what is prescribed in the rubrics of the Office. The bell for the Vespers of the Dead is rung from the time they begin until the *De Profundis;* if there is no sermon, it should be rung from the *Magnificat* to the antiphon *Placebo*. If there is a sermon on All Saints' day, it will be well to have it between the two Vespers.

When the feast of All Saints falls on a Saturday, the Office of the Dead is transferred to the following Monday, and in that case the Vespers of the Dead are said after those of the Sunday—following in this the custom of the place. After the evening *Angelus*, a peal is rung for a quarter of an hour; another about seven o'clock, and again after Matins. At the *Benedictus* of our Lady's Office, the bell is rung for Matins of the Dead, until they commence. The next morning a peal is rung for a quarter of an hour after the *Angelus*.

At Vespers and Matins of the Office of the Blessed Virgin, the Superior's chanters and chorists take their ordinary places near her, and in order to make no disorder, the chorists are chanters.

After the *Benedicamus Domino* of Lauds of the Office of the Blessed Virgin, Matins for the Dead are said. When the Sister who officiates says *Per Dominum* of the last prayer, the Superior's chanters go to the middle of the choir to say the Invitatory, *Regem cui omnia vivunt*, and the *Venite*. The first chorist intones the first antiphon, the chanter the psalm. The antiphons are doubled, they do not ask the Blessing before the lessons, nor say *Tu autem* after, but the last word is said quite slowly, and at once the choir takes up the response that follows the lesson.

They do the same at the second nocturn, which falls to the Assistant's choir. The third nocturn returns to that of the Superior.

The chorists go out to say the versicle, when the last verse of the third psalm of each nocturn is begun, and at Lauds at the end of the last psalm.

At the mid-day Obedience, the Assistant names two Sisters of each choir to read the three lessons of the first nocturn, and the first of the second; the chorists say the two last, and the chanters the two first of the third nocturn; the Superior says the last.

Those who have been named to say the first lesson of each nocturn, go out at the end of the last psalm to say their lesson; at the end they wait to say the versicle of the response; she who has to read the following lesson, goes out at the beginning of the response to say the versicle with her who has said the preceding lesson. At the end of the ninth lesson, the chanters say with the Superior the versicle of the response *Libera me Domine*, which is proper to this day.

At the end of Mass the four Little Hours are said in succession, and immediately before the High Mass Lauds are said. The bell is rung for a good half quarter of an hour before assembling in the choir, and as soon as the sign is given, the first chorist intones the antiphon *Exultabunt* and the chanter the psalm *Miserere*, and thus consecutively; this is a general rule when the three nocturns are said. At other services for the Dead, None is said before the High Mass. The bell is rung for Mass at the psalm *Deus, Deus meus* to the end of the canticle *Ego dixi*, and is tolled during ten or twelve verses of the *Laudate*, the last bell being tolled at the *Benedictus*. The bell is also rung for the *Libera*, which is sung after Mass.

The Religious of the choir who have not assisted at the Office of the Dead on this day should say it in private.

After the Vespers of this day, it is the custom to go in procession to the cemetery, saying the seven Penitential Psalms; they are commenced in the choir. After the *Benedicamus Domino*, the Sister who officiates intones the antiphon *Ne reminiscaris*, and the two chanters the psalm *Domine ne in furore;* if the Superior pleases, the *Libera* is sung at the cemetery; the chanters begin it and say the versicles; at the end the Superior says *Kyrie eleison*, &c., *Pater noster*, and *Et ne nos inducas*, &c., *A porta inferi*, and the prayer *Fidelium*, with the two versicles which follow. The chanters take up the psalms where they had left off. *Gloria Patri* is not said at the end, only *Requiem* after the last.

The Sisters do not wear mantles for this procession. If they cannot go to the cemetery, the seven psalms are said in choir.

In France the Sunday which follows the octave of the feast of All Saints, the FEAST OF THE DEDICATION OF THE CHURCHES is celebrated; it is first class, with octave; the first Vespers are sung, with the ceremonies of great feasts, and the Superior officiates. Convents established out of France will keep the feast according to the custom of the place.

21st. FEAST OF THE PRESENTATION OF OUR LADY, holiday of Rule. It is kept as a feast of the second class, but the Superior officiates.

During the three days of retreat which precede this feast, the Assistant fastens the formula for the renewal of vows to the screen in the choir.

On the feast, the Blessed Sacrament being exposed after High Mass, the Sisters approach the grate, and one after another in rank of profession they renew their vows, in presence of the Celebrant, in the following manner, their right hand on the Holy Gospel, and the hymn, *Quam pulchre graditur, Filia principis* being sung.

Formula of the renewal of Vows.

I, Sister Mary N. of N., confirm and renew with my whole heart, the vows which I have made to my God, to serve Him for ever (or for one year) in the Congregation of Our Lady of Charity of the Good Shepherd of Angers, by Obedience, Chastity, and Poverty, and to labour for the salvation of the souls of the persons who enter this house to be converted, in the name of the Father, and of the Son, and of the Holy Ghost, and in honour of the Most Holy Virgin, Mother of this Congregation. *Amen.*

The Sister Tourières renew their vow of Obedience or their vows after the Lay Sisters as follows:

Formula of the renewal of Vows of the Sister Tourières.

I, Sister Mary N. N., confirm and renew with my whole heart (if they have not made perpetual vows, they add: for one year), the vows of Obedience, Chastity, and Poverty, which I have made to my God: in the name of the Father, and of the Son, and of the Holy Ghost, and in honour of the Most Blessed Virgin, Mother of this Congregation. *Amen.*

At the end of the renewal the *Te Deum* is sung in thanksgiving, during which the Kiss of Peace is given.

The Sister Assistant takes care to put in the Community Room what is necessary for the Sisters to write their Renewal. She writes, or has it written for those who cannot do so; the Superior or the Assistant signs it. She takes care that this book is kept in good condition, and not blotted; she removes it after the Sisters have written in it. Those prevented by illness from renewing their vows on this day, cannot do so in public after the day has passed.

During dinner the *Wishes* of our Venerable Father Eudes, which are at the beginning of our holy Constitutions, are read in the Refectory.

25th. THE FEAST OF SAINT CATHERINE, virgin and martyr, holiday of rule. The intention of the Holy Communion shall be in thanksgiving that on this day, in the year 1641, our Congregation was first begun.

DECEMBER.

3rd. FEAST OF SAINT FRANCIS XAVIER. The intention of the Holy Communion will be to obtain a spirit of zeal for the salvation of souls.

8th. THE FEAST OF THE IMMACULATE CONCEPTION, double of the first class, with an octave.

The Convents which have the devotion to say or sing the Office of the Immaculate Conception during the octave, may do so after obedience, or at any hour the Superior pleases. She begins it in her place; the first chanter intones the first hymn and says the first prayer, the second chanter intones the second hymn and says the prayer, and so on alternately. The chorists say their versicles, without leaving their places. The Superior begins the antiphon *Hæc est virgo*, and says the versicle and prayer which follow. The choir does not incline at the prayers.

25th. THE NATIVITY OF OUR LORD, double of the first class, with an octave. On the Eve the Sisters do not work at the evening recreation. The Superior invites them to draw the Offices of the Court of King Jesus.

At half-past seven the Epistles and Gospels of the feast are read, afterwards the bell is rung for the obedience, and all go to the choir to make the examen, and read the point of meditation. The Sisters who wish to do so retire to rest, and those who do not should be most careful to observe great tranquillity. At half-past eight four strokes are rung for the silence.

At ten o'clock, Matins are said. The first Nocturn is sung (the choir is seated while the versicles of the responses are sung at Matins); the second and third Nocturns are in Psalmody. Then the Holy Mass is sung, at which there is a general Communion. After High Mass Lauds are recited, the *Benedictus* is sung. The bell is rung during the whole of the *Gloria in excelsis* at Midnight Mass.

The signal for rising in the morning is given at half-past six, Prime is said at seven, followed by the Mass of the Aurora; the Sisters assist at it, then withdraw till Terce, which is sung at half-past eight ; after None Mass is sung, at the end of which the Kiss of Peace is given.

Matins are said earlier than usual, as the Sisters have watched a good deal the preceding night.

Movable Feasts.

Advent.

The first Sunday of Advent is always that which is nearest to the feast of Saint Andrew, so that if Saint Andrew fall on Monday, Tuesday, or Wednesday, the Sunday which precedes this feast is the first Sunday of Advent. If the feast fall on Thursday, Friday, or Saturday, the following Sunday is the first of Advent; if it fall on Sunday, this day itself is the first Sunday of Advent; in this case the commemoration of Saint Andrew is transferred to the following day.

Septuagesima.

At the Vespers of the Saturday before Septuagesima, after the *Benedicamus Domino*, *Alleluia* is said twice, and the same at the response; from then until Vespers of Holy Saturday the *Alleluias* are omitted; *Laus tibi Domine*, &c., is said instead.

When Septuagesima falls on the first Sunday after the octave of the Epiphany, on the first Saturday after the octave, which is not occupied by a double, or the first day after the octave, commemoration of the second Sunday after the Epiphany is made. The feasts which fall on Septuagesima and the two following Sundays are transferred to the first vacant day, except the feast of the Most Holy Heart of the Blessed Virgin, Titular of this Congregation, that of the Patron, or that of the Dedication of the Church.

The Forty Hours.

When the devotion of the Forty Hours' Exposition of the Blessed Sacrament takes place on the three days which precede Ash Wednesday, the Masses are sung according to the custom of the Diocese.

These three days Vespers are sung, the *Nunc dimittis* at Compline, and in the evening at Benediction the psalm *Miserere* for sinners.

Ash Wednesday.

The intention of the Holy Communion will be for the Lenten preachers. The Meditations, until Friday morning, are on death, afterwards they should be on the Passion of our Lord, or on the Gospels. At the end of None, the Celebrant goes up to the altar and the chanters intone the anthem *Exaudi nos Domine*, which the choir continues; after the *Gloria Patri*, the anthem is repeated as in an Introit; when the Priest says the fourth prayer of the blessing of the ashes, which begins by these words *Omnipotens sempiterne Deus, qui Ninivitis*, the Superior and Assistant go to the grate for Communion to receive them on the head, the other Sisters follow, two and two, observing the ceremonies prescribed for the feast of the Purification.

Immediately the Priest begins the distribution of the ashes, the chanters intone the antiphons marked in the Gradual, namely: *Immutemur habitu, Inter vestibulum*, and the response *Emendemus*, which the choir continues; they are repeated until the end of the distribution, continuing while they are given to the Penitents. The *Gloria Patri* is kept for the end, and after it is said, *Attende Domine* is repeated; then the choir turns to the altar and answers the Celebrant when he says the prayer *Concede*. At the end the Sisters kneel down to hear Holy Mass.

The ashes must be made from the palms of the preceding year, without mixture of any other wood.

Note.—During Lent, and in general on other fasting days, the grace of supper is said at dinner; at collation only an *Ave Maria* is said, with the sign of the Cross at the end, and the Reader does not ask the blessing.

From the first Friday of Lent inclusively, until Wednesday in Holy Week exclusively, the *Stabat* is sung every

c

day, with the versicle and prayer for the feast of Our Lady of Dolours (Friday in Passion Week). At the beginning of the anthem of the Blessed Virgin, which is said at the end of Compline, two strokes are rung on the Church bell for the *Stabat*, and four strokes at twice when the Litany is begun, as usual.

From the first Saturday of Lent, Vespers are said in the morning. The first bell is rung at a quarter-past ten and the second at half-past ten.—In Lent, Vespers may not be said in choir before ten o'clock in the morning, and at other times not before two o'clock in the afternoon.

At the Mass of the Ferias, when the Priest says the versicle, *Adjuva nos*, making a genuflexion, the Sisters kneel during the whole of the versicle.

PALM SUNDAY.

Terce, Sext, and None are said at a quarter to eight; at the end, the Celebrant, in purple cope, or at least purple stole, accompanied by his Ministers, also in suitable vestments, come to the altar to bless the palms. When he reaches the step of the altar, the Sister Sacristan makes a sign to the chanters to intone *Hosanna filio David*, which the choir continues. The Celebrant says the prayer, during which the Religious stand facing the altar; they sit down during the Epistle; when it is finished they sing the response, *In Monte Oliveti* or *Collegerunt*, as in the Gradual. They answer the prayers which the Celebrant says, and also the Preface, observing to follow the tone he takes, and to sing the *Sanctus* in the Ferial tone. After the *Sanctus*, the Convent bell is rung to give notice to the absent to come to the distribution and procession.

At the sixth prayer, which begins *Deus qui Filium tuum Jesum Christum*, which is the last of the blessing, the Superior and Assistant go to the Communion grate to receive their palm; the other Religious follow in rank two and two with the same ceremonies as prescribed for receiving the candles. When the Priest receives his palm from the deacon, the chanters intone the anthems *Pueri Hebræorum*, which the choir continues; they are repeated to the end of the distribution, after which the choir turns towards the altar and answers the Priest at the last prayer. As soon as the prayer is begun, the Sisters who carry the cross and candlesticks put down their palms and stand in the middle of the choir, in order that after the deacon has sung *Procedamus in pace*, and that the choir has answered *In nomine Christi, Amen*, they may set out to begin the procession; all follow in good order, holding the palm in the left hand, if they are on the Superior's choir, and in the right hand if they are on the Assistant's. The chanters intone the antiphon *Cum appropinquaret* and the others, as they are in the Gradual, repeating or retrenching according to the length of the procession, which in passing through the cloisters does not stop at the altar. When the cross-bearer re-enters the choir, the chanters intone the anthem *Ingrediente Domino*, after which the cross and candlesticks are put back in their places and the Mass begins.

They hold their palms to the end of the Passion, because this ceremony signifies that the ignominy of the Passion is our victory.

In Communities where they have the devotion to sing the *Gloria laus*, with the ceremonies prescribed in the Roman Missal, at the return of the procession, two or four chanters will enter the choir, and having shut the door, they stand facing the procession. They sing the *Gloria laus*, the choir repeats it outside the closed doors, those who are inside sing *Israel es tu*, and the following verses, all or in part, as is thought best; those who are outside repeat *Gloria laus* at the end of each verse. When the Superior thinks it time to enter, she gives the sign; the cross-bearer knocks three times at the first door on the right side, which she does with the foot of the cross; at once the chanters open and retire to their places, the procession enters singing *Ingrediente Domino*, as in the Missal.

The crucifix carried in this procession should be covered with purple. The Sisters genuflect at the words of Saint Paul, *Ut in nomine Jesu*, &c., which are in the Epistle of this day.

THE THREE DAYS OF TENEBRÆ.

On Wednesday in Holy Week, the bell for spiritual reading is rung at two o'clock, that for Compline at three; at the end the Litany is said, omitting the *Stabat*. The bell for meditation is rung at the beginning of the Litany, as usual; shortly before it ends, the first bell is rung for Tenebræ and the last is rung at four o'clock.

These three days the Divine Office is said, as in the Holy Week books; it is commenced on Wednesday by Matins of the following day.—Those who, through weakness or for some other reason, cannot say the Divine Office, recite that of the Blessed Virgin, with the Superior's permission. They double the anthems. On the three last days of Holy Week, it is forbidden to say publicly in choir the Office of the Blessed Virgin.

The anthems are doubled and intoned as they are in the Holy Week books, and not as far as the commas, if these are too distant.

Only the first Nocturn is sung, with the Lamentations or Lessons, and the three responses are in the ordinary chant.

At Lauds the *Benedictus* anthem is sung, with the verse *Christus factus est.* The *Gloria Patri* is not said at the end of the psalms, but they are finished rather slowly.— The Sister Sacristan places the triangular candlestick in the choir, near the grate on the Epistle side, with fifteen candles, yellow or white, according to the custom of the place.

Matins.

At Matins, the Superior, standing in her stall, and having said the *Pater*, *Ave*, and *Credo*, makes the sign of the Cross, the choir does the same. She intones the anthem, *Zelus domus tuæ*, and the chanter the psalm *Salvum me fac Deus*, and thus consecutively from choir to choir. (The Religious do not take mantles for Tenebræ.) The second Nocturn falls to the Assistant's choir; the chorist begins the first anthem, the chanter the first psalm.

The third Nocturn returns to the Superior's choir, the chorist begins the first anthem, and the chanters the psalms which fall to them.

The chorists go to say the versicles at the beginning of the last verse of the last psalm of each Nocturn. The same is observed at Lauds. Those who are named to say the first lessons of the two first Nocturns, go out at the end of the last verse of the third psalm.

On these three days the Blessing is not asked at the beginning, nor *Tu autem* said at the end of the lessons, but before the first lesson of each Nocturn they merely say the *Pater* in secret, at the end of which the Superior gives the sign to begin the first lesson, the other two are said after the response, and all are finished rather slowly.

At the end of each lesson of the first Nocturn, the Sisters who sing at the lectern, go to the middle of the choir to sing the response, which the chanters begin.

The choir is seated during the versicles of the responses at the first Nocturn; those who sing the Lamentations may sit down if they wish, and for this purpose the Assistant has a chair placed above the lectern.

Those who say the second and third lessons of the two first Nocturns, go out when the choir commences the response which precedes the lesson they have to read, and join her who has said the lesson, to assist in saying the versicle. She who has said the second lesson comes back to say the versicle with her who has said the third lesson, and both retire after having said the versicle which follows the lesson. The chorists say the two last of the second Nocturn. The chanters say the two first of the last Nocturn, and go out together at the end of the last psalm. After having said their lessons they wait for the Superior, who comes to say the last, they say the versicle with her, all three genuflect together, and retire.

Lauds.

At Lauds, the first chorist intones the first antiphon, and the chanter the first psalm. At the antiphon which follows the *Benedictus*, the Sisters place themselves on their knees in front of the *Marchepied;* the Superior, in front of the *Marchepied* of her stall, begins the verse *Christus factus est*, the chanters kneeling a little behind her.

The *Pater* is said in secret; the Superior gives the sign and the chanters begin the *Miserere* in a soft and moderate tone; afterwards the Superior, inclining her head a little, says the *Respice*, finishing by the words: *Crucis subire tormentum*, the rest is said in secret. At the end the Superior knocks upon her book, and a noise is made which should not be long nor rough.

Before and after collation, the verse *Christus factus est* is said. The Reader begins without saying *In nomine Domini*, or the title, and she finishes without saying the *Tu autem* at the end. She does not read the Constitutions on these days, nor the Rule, nor the Martyrology; neither are the *Ave Cor*, the *Ave Maria filia Dei Patris*, nor the *Angelus* said aloud.

Obedience is rung half a quarter of an hour before half-past eight, as usual. At the half hour four strokes are rung on the Church bell for silence. The Community goes to the choir to say a few prayers and make the examen. The point of meditation is read without a title, and at nine o'clock the Superior gives the blessing in secret, and all retire.

Maundy Thursday.

On this day and the two following, the *Veni Sancte Spiritus* is not said before the morning meditation.

Prime.

Prime is said at the usual hour; after the *Pater*, *Ave*, and *Credo*, which are said in secret, all make the sign of the Cross; the Superior gives the sign, and the first chanter in her stall begins the *Deus in nomine*, &c. At the end of each hour the Superior begins in a low voice the versicle *Christus factus est*, which the choir continues; after the *Pater*, which is said in secret, the chanter begins the *Miserere*, and the Superior says the *Respice* as before.

Terce, Sext, None, and Vespers.

At half-past eight, Terce, Sext, and None are said; after the *Pater* and *Ave* all make the sign of the Cross, the Superior gives the sign, and the first chanter begins the first psalm and the others that follow.

After None, High Mass begins. At the *Gloria in excelsis* the bells are rung. From this time they are not rung until the *Gloria in excelsis* on Holy Saturday; the signal for the exercises is given with the *crécelle*. The organ is also silent during this time. Although the Mass on Holy Thursday is solemn, there is no singing at the Elevation.

After the Communion the Celebrant places the Sacred Host in the Chalice, and covers it with the Pall, the Paten, and the Veil. After Mass he incenses the Blessed Sacrament, ties the Veil with a white ribbon, and, holding the Chalice in his hand, with his back to the altar, he proceeds to the Altar of Repose, the choir singing the *Pange lingua*.

While the signal for the Office, &c., is given with the *crécelle*, the Sisters do not assemble in the ante-choir, they go direct to the choir. No bell shall be rung to call the Sisters on these two days.

At Vespers, which follow immediately, the Superior in her stall begins the first antiphon, also the one at the *Magnificat*.

After Vespers the Clergy strip the Altar, during which the Sisters say alternately the psalm, *Deus, Deus meus, respice in me*.

It is to be remarked that as soon as the Blessed Sacrament is deposited in the place which has been prepared, until It is replaced in the Tabernacle, the Sisters (wearing their mantles), two and two, shall by turn be in adoration, and during these two days they are at liberty not to work, so as to remain before the Blessed Sacrament.

The ceremony of the Mandatum.

About two o'clock in the afternoon the Sisters assemble in the Community Room; they begin the ceremony by the antiphon *Mandatum novum*, which is sung kneeling. When the chanters intone the psalm *Beati immaculati in via*, the Sisters stand. The Superior takes off her mantle; the linen is brought to her, and the first chanter girds her to perform the ceremony, at which, if it can be, two Lay Sisters assist her; the one going before her carries an earthenware jug and basin, with water, of which she pours a little on each foot, the other Sister carries a towel on her arm, and follows the Superior; the latter begins with the Assistant (who sits down, which the others do two at a time); she then goes to the first in rank on the same side, placing herself on her knees before them, washes their right foot, wipes it with the linen which the Sister gives her, and kisses it. During this time the antiphons which are in the Gradual are sung alternately, *Mandatum novum do vobis* being repeated, which the chanters intone; the choir takes up *Ut diligatis invicem*, &c. They begin all the antiphons and the psalms, which the choir continues, as in the Holy Week books. If it be necessary to repeat the antiphons already said, the chanters take care that this repetition is made before saying the versicle *Simul quoque cum Beatis*, because it must be kept with what follows to be said when the Superior washes her hands.

The Superior having taken off the linen and put on her mantle, goes to her own place; the Sisters kneel, a few prayers are said, the sign is given, and all retire.

The two first Mistresses of the Magdalens and Penitents then begin in their quarters the ceremony of the *Mandatum*, assisted by two Lay Sisters, whom the Assistant should have named.

Compline.

Compline is begun on these two days by the *Confiteor*, which the Superior says in her stall, standing and inclining; the Sisters turn in choir when she begins it; afterwards they say the *Misereatur* and *Confiteor* as usual; the Superior takes up the *Misereatur* and says the *Indulgentiam;* after the choir has answered the last *Amen*, the chanter begins the psalm *Cum invocarem*, &c. On these two days neither the Litany nor the *Stabat* is said after Compline.

The evening Obedience is held at eight o'clock, after which the Community goes to the choir to sing the *Stabat*. The Adoration of the Blessed Sacrament is divided amongst the Sisters. Those who rise in the night are free to go to bed after their examen, or even sooner, if they wish.

On Holy Thursday and Good Friday, no sign is given for the silence at night, as the Sisters are in the choir or in their cells.

Good Friday.

On the morning of this day, Prime, Terce, Sext, and None are said consecutively, after which there is, if possible, a sermon on the Passion, followed by the service of the Altar proper to the day.

Should the community leave the choir, *Blessed be God* is not said. The same is observed on the following day.

During the Lesson and Epistle, which are read before the Passion, the Sisters are seated in their stalls, a little turned towards the altar; at the end they sing the Tracts, sitting down after the first verse has been intoned, they stand during the prayers, to which they answer *Amen*, and genuflect when *Flectamus genua* is said, rising at *Levate*.

When the Celebrant says *Ecce lignum crucis*, they answer *Venite adoremus* three times, raising the tone higher as the Celebrant ought to do, and genuflecting each time.

The Adoration of the Cross.

The Sister Sacristan prepares beforehand in the middle of the choir a cushion on which she places a crucifix. When the Celebrant begins the Adoration, the Sisters rise and very quietly place themselves in order at the lower end of the choir for the Adoration; the Superior begins and the others follow in their rank, two and two. They take off their shoes and make three genuflexions on both knees, as they go, noticing carefully the distances and their steps, so that at the time she who precedes has finished the Adoration, she who follows is ready to make it. During the Adoration the whole or part of what is prescribed in the Roman Gradual is sung, according to the number of those who go to adore, terminating by the *Dulce lignum.*

The Adoration being finished, the candles are lighted, and the rest of the ceremony proceeded with. The Celebrant having removed the Blessed Sacrament from the Altar of Repose, the *Vexilla Regis* is intoned, the Sisters singing it alternately with the Ecclesiastics. The hymn ended, they remain kneeling, to answer the Priest when he says the *Pater Noster*, and the prayer which follows it.

When the Celebrant has left the Altar, the Superior gives the sign, all rise without kissing the ground, she begins the first antiphon of Vespers and the chanter the first psalm.

The Stations.

It is the custom to make the seven Stations all together after the mid-day Obedience, or during the evening recreation, or any other hour, as the Superior shall consider most convenient.

The two chanters of the procession say the Seven Penitential Psalms; the Community answers to each verse of the psalms, *Miserere mei secundum magnam*, &c. Before reading each Station, the anthem *Adoramus te Christe* is said, and after it they say five *Paters* and *Aves*.

The Obedience is held at seven o'clock; afterwards the Sisters go to the choir to make the examen and read the point of Meditation, so as to retire earlier than on the preceding days.

HOLY SATURDAY.

Prime is said after Meditation.

At eight o'clock in the morning Terce, Sext, and None are said, afterwards the Celebrant, in alb, stole and violet cope, blesses the new fire at the door of the Church; he then returns to the Altar. When the deacon sings *Lumen Christi*, the Sisters, kneeling, answer *Deo Gratias*, raising the tone three times, in proportion as he raises it. The Sisters stand when the deacon begins *Exultet jam angelica*, and pay attention to answer at the right moment. They sit down during the Prophecies, a little turned towards the Altar, and rise at the end of each, doing so a little before the end of those after which they are to sing the Tract, to begin immediately they are finished. They genuflect when *Flectamus genua* is said, and answer *Amen* at the end of the prayers, after the last they kneel to sing the Litany of the Saints; they are doubled as far as the versicle *Christe exaudi nos* at the end, after which the chanters of the Mass solemnly intone the *Kyrie eleison*, and the rest of the Mass is continued in the same manner. The first signal for Mass is given with the *crécelle* at the ninth prophecy, and the last at the twelfth.

When the Celebrant intones the *Gloria in excelsis*, the bells are rung as on Maundy Thursday.[1] When he says *Alleluia*, the Sisters answer in the same tone, raising it in proportion as he does, according to the Gradual.

After the Communion the Superior and her chanters go to the middle of the choir; all rise and take their places turned towards the Altar. The Superior intones the first *Alleluia* of Vespers, the choir says the two others; the chanters intone the *Laudate Dominum omnes gentes*, afterwards they all three genuflect together, and return to their places. The chanter takes up the *Alleluia* and the Celebrant begins the antiphon *Vespere*, which the choir continues, the chanter intones the *Magnificat*. The Sisters remain turned towards the Altar during the psalm *Laudate Dominum omnes gentes*, and also for the *Magnificat*. (It is a general rule that the Sisters turn in choir every time they say a verse during which they ought to incline, unless it is prescribed otherwise.) They kneel to receive the blessing at the end of Mass.

The spiritual reading is at three o'clock.

At Compline the first chorist goes above the lectern to say the short lesson, with the ceremonies observed for the feast of the Most Pure Heart of Mary. The Superior

---

[1] The bells should not ring before those of the Cathedral.

intones the antiphon *Vespere* before the *Nunc Dimittis*. The Divine Office for Easter is said as in the Breviary. At Matins the chanter intones the antiphon *Hæc dies* before the *Benedictus*. The choir turns to the Altar for the *Hæc dies*, which takes the place of the Little Chapter.

EASTER SUNDAY.

This feast is most solemn, and is of first class. The Kiss of Peace is given.

At Compline the Superior says the first *Alleluia* before the *Nunc dimittis*.

The Office of the third feast is not sung.

NOTICE FOR THE PASCHAL TIME.

From Compline of Easter Sunday, until None of the Eve of the feast of the Blessed Trinity inclusively, *Alleluia* is said after the antiphons, versicles, responses, and invitatory. During the octave of the feast of Easter, after the *Benedicamus Domino* of Lauds, as well as of Vespers, two *Alleluias* are added, until the first Vespers of Low Sunday exclusively.

The chanters ought not to add *Alleluia* when they take up the invitatory *Ave Maria*, which is said after the *Gloria Patri* of the *Venite*, because the choir says it in answering *Dominus tecum;* neither should the chorists add *Alleluia* to the versicles which follow the lessons at Matins; but it is added to the responses.

Alleluia is not added to the prayers which are not part of the Office, for example, after the versicle of the *Veni Sancte* or the Litany.

From this day until the feast of the Most Holy Trinity, the hymns of the Office and the *Regina Cœli* are said standing (the Sisters kneel nevertheless for the first verse of the *Ave Maris Stella*); this is observed for all the great anthems at the end of the Office, they must be said standing from the Vespers of Saturday, until the end of Compline, on all Sundays in the year.[1]

At the end of the Gospel on the feast of the Ascension, the Paschal Candle is extinguished; it ought to be lighted during Mass and solemn Vespers, on Holy Saturday, Easter Sunday, and the two following days, as well as all Sundays; but not on other feasts.

The Office for the Dead is not said during Paschal time. It is said after the feast of the Most Holy Trinity, on the first day that is not a double.

When prayers are said for the necessities of the Church during Paschal Time, *Alleluia* is not added.

Feasts which fall during Paschal Time.

The second Sunday after Easter, the feast of Our Lady Mother of the Good Shepherd is celebrated, and the Office proper to the day is said.

At Matins, as the three psalms are said under one antiphon, when the psalms end on the Superior's choir, the psalm which follows should commence on the Assistant's choir, and vice-versa.

On the three Rogation days the procession is made and the Litany of the Saints is sung as on Saint Mark's day; the *Ut fructus terræ dare* is repeated twice, and the third day *Per Ascensionem tuam* is also said twice.

On the feast of the Ascension the Community assembles in the choir at noon to sing the hymn *Salutis humanæ Sator*, after which the Superior says aloud, or causes to be said, the prayer to Jesus Christ, which is at the end of the Spiritual Exercises.

At the end of the first Vespers of Pentecost, the bell is tolled five times, to give notice to the absent to come to draw the Gifts of the Holy Ghost, as has been said for the Beatitudes.

The Office of Pentecost is proper to the day, and after Mass the Kiss of Peace is given.

---

[1] During Paschal time, when there is a procession, the Litany of the Blessed Virgin must be commenced standing.

The Feast of Corpus Christi.

After the Mass, which is sung solemnly, the Sisters rise to sing the *Laudate* with the *Alleluias*.

In houses where there is a convenient place for it, there shall be a procession of the Blessed Sacrament, following the custom of the diocese.

During the octave, the Blessed Sacrament is exposed after Mass; neither the Mass nor the *Laudate* are sung. The bell is not rung for the Exposition of the Blessed Sacrament, but if It is exposed without Mass being said, the bell is tolled five times towards the end of Prime, to assemble the Community in the choir.

The Sisters (wearing mantles) must be in adoration, at least two at a time, out of the times of the Office and Meditation. A little before the end of each half hour, the younger of the two Sisters tolls the bell twice, to call those who are to follow.

Vespers and the *Nunc dimittis* are sung every day of the octave. After Compline, Benediction is given, the bell for which is rung from the second psalm of Compline until the *Nunc dimittis*.

In houses where it would be difficult to have Exposition of the Blessed Sacrament during the octave, there ought to be Benediction in the evening.

The first Friday after the octave of Corpus Christi, the feast of the Sacred Heart of Jesus is celebrated. The Blessed Sacrament is exposed all day, and during the octave from Vespers to Compline. The Office is proper to the day.

Ceremonial of the Choir.

OF ENTERING THE CHOIR FOR THE OFFICE.

The Sisters assemble in the ante-choir a little before Terce, Vespers, and Compline, so that at the first sound of the bell, they can enter the choir; the chanters, chorists, and those who have particular places, take the rank that they are to hold in the choir; before entering, all turn a little towards the Superior or the Assistant, to make an inclination; they do the same in passing the holy Relics, if there are any.

They enter the choir in order, two and two, with gravity and modesty, make an inclination to the statue of our Lady, which is above the Superior's stall, and, having advanced towards the middle of the choir, genuflect to the Blessed Sacrament, distant from one another one step; at the same time the two who follow make the inclination, and so on consecutively. If the convenience of the place will not allow them to do this, they may first make the genuflection to the Blessed Sacrament, and the inclination to the Superior in taking their places. She who is to officiate places herself in the middle of the choir before the lectern. When the sign is given to begin the Office, they kiss the ground all together, and rise quietly and promptly.—They ought to wait the space of a *Pater* and *Ave* after the bell has ceased ringing, before the sign is given to begin the Office, if the Superior is absent, unless they are quite sure she is not coming.

Remark.—During retreats and when the Blessed Sacrament is exposed, the Sisters enter the choir direct without assembling in the ante-choir, and in winter when the Angelus is rung before Compline they do the same.

OF THE SISTER WHO OFFICIATES.

She begins her week at Vespers on Saturday, and finishes at None of the following Saturday inclusively.

She asks a blessing of the Superior or Assistant before beginning her week; if they are not in the choir at the commencement of Vespers, she asks it before going to say the Little Chapter or the Prayer, or else she waits for the first Office at which they assist. To receive it she kneels down and inclines, with her hands joined, before the Superior (or Assistant in her absence), who rises, and, making the sign of the Cross over her, says: *Benedicat te* † *Pater et Filius et Spiritus Sanctus. Amen.* If the Superior is not at Vespers, although the blessing has been given by the Assistant, the officiant nevertheless asks it of the Superior at Compline, or else in the evening before saying the versicle and prayer of the *Inviolata*, and even on Sunday morning at Prime.

She ought to know exactly what she has to say, and foresee it, especially the extra Offices; as far as can be, she shall not undertake to say anything by heart.

The sign being given to commence the Office, she intones *Ave Maria*, which is said in secret; she begins *Deus in adjutorium*, &c., the choir answers *Domine ad adjuvandum;* when they begin *Alleluia*, or *Laus tibi Domine*, she genuflects and retires to her stall. Every time she goes out to officiate, she makes an inclination to the Superior; at the lectern she genuflects before beginning, after she has finished she makes another genuflection, and the inclination to the Superior as she returns to her stall.

At Matins she goes to the middle of the choir to say the *Precibus*, when *Et in sæcula* of the *Gloria Patri* of the last psalm is said. After the response to the versicle she begins the *Pater*, which the choir says in secret; she says aloud *Et ne nos inducas*, &c., and begins the *Precibus*. She gives the blessing of the first lesson and returns to her stall, from whence she gives the blessing of the two other lessons,[1] and says the *Deus in adjutorium* at Lauds. She begins the antiphons of the *Benedictus*, *Magnificat*, and *Nunc Dimittis*, making an inclination of her head after.

At the end of the last psalm of every hour (except Compline), when *Et in sæcula* of the *Gloria Patri* is said, she goes to the lectern to say the Chapter. At the four Little Hours, she remains to say the prayer and versicle which follow it; she goes in the same way at the end of the *Benedictus* and *Magnificat*, to say the prayers of Lauds and Vespers. She goes to say the chapter of Compline, when *Jesu tibi sit gloria* of the *Memento* is said, and then retires to her place. When *Et in sæcula* of the *Gloria Patri* of the *Nunc dimittis* is said, she returns to say the prayer and the rest.

When she has said *Benedicamus Domino*, she turns a little towards the Superior to receive the blessing, observing not to turn her back to the Blessed Sacrament. In the absence of the Superior and the Assistant, she gives the blessing, making the sign of the Cross on herself, the Sisters do the same without inclining or turning in choir. The Sister who officiates ought to say the whole in the middle of the choir and standing, as also the versicle and prayer, which follow the anthem of the Blessed Virgin, which is said at the end of the Office, although the said anthem may have been recited kneeling.—When a novice officiates, and that the Superior and Assistant are not at Compline to give the blessing, the Surveillante, or the oldest professed, ought to go to the lectern to say the prayer; she observes what is said above.

Immediately after the *Pater*, which is said in secret (excepting at Compline, when it is not said), she intones *Dominus det nobis suam pacem* in psalmody, whether the anthem of the Blessed Virgin is sung or not. This anthem is not sung except after Compline. If the anthem is sung she also sings the versicle and prayer which follow. The

---

[1] When a novice officiates at Matins, the Superior gives the blessing; if she and the Assistant are absent, it is given by the Surveillante, or the oldest professed Sister.

D

Divinum auxilium is always said in psalmody, but in a rather lower tone.[1]

After the final anthem at Compline, she says the Litany of the Blessed Virgin, kneeling in the middle of the choir, and the versicle and prayer standing; the same for the versicle and prayer of the *Stabat*.

After the last *Amen* at Lauds, she begins the *Ave Maria*, which is said for Benefactors; she then genuflects and retires to her place, when she begins the *Ave Cor Sanctissimum*, which is said in honour of the Sacred Hearts of Jesus and Mary, and to ask for union amongst the houses of the Institute, then the *Veni Sancte Spiritus*, and the versicle *Emitte Spiritum tuum*, and three times *A subitanea*, &c.

In the morning after the point of Meditation has been read, she begins the *Veni Sancte Spiritus*, says the versicle and prayer, then *Our Lady of Charity*, &c., and *Monstra te*, &c.

When the bell for Prime is rung she ought to place herself before the lectern, ready to begin; at the end she commences the *Ave Maria, filia Dei Patris*, which is said for the conversion of the Penitents.

When extra prayers are said for a certain time, the Sister who officiates should begin them, and say the versicles and prayers, if there are any; but if it is only for a few days, the Superior should do so.

If through inadvertence, she says the wrong prayer, she ought to be allowed to continue, but the Sisters say to themselves what she ought to have said.

OF THE FIRST CHANTER.

She ought to begin as far as the mediant the hymns, psalms, and canticles, which belong to her choir. She intones the *Kyrie eleison*, which precedes the prayers of the Office, says the *Venite* at Matins, and goes to say the last lesson a little before the versicle of the response of the

---

[1] At Compline of the Divine Office only the Superior and Assistant may say the *Confiteor* in their stalls; the other Sisters who officiate go to the lectern.

second is begun, and remains two steps distant from the chorist; when they have said the versicle and finished the response, she says *Jube Domine, benedicere*, inclining to the Sister who officiates to receive the blessing; then she begins the lesson. When she says *Tu autem*, she inclines profoundly, afterwards she intones the *Te Deum*, makes the genuflection to the Blessed Sacrament, and the inclination to the Superior as she takes her place again.

If the *Te Deum* is not said, she remains to say the versicle of the response and the *Gloria Patri*, as far as the *Sancto*, after which she retires.

She leaves to go and say the *Benedicamus Domino* of Vespers with the other chanter, when the Sister who officiates says *Per Dominum* of the last prayer, making together the inclination to the Superior; and when they are two steps above the lectern they genuflect to the Blessed Sacrament, being two steps distant from one another. Returning they observe the same ceremony.

She intones the *Magnificat*, which is sung, although the Office is being said in psalmody, except in Lent, when she only begins it in a rather higher tone.

She who has been first chanter officiates the first time the Office returns to her choir.

Of the Second Chanter.

She begins the psalms which fall to her choir. She goes to say the *Benedicamus Domino* of Vespers with the other chanter, making together the ceremonies prescribed above.

Those who have officiated one week are second chanters the following week. The chanters take the places nearest to the stall of the Superior, if nothing prevent it.

Of the First Chorist.

She says all the versicles, excepting those which fall to the Sister who officiates, and she intones the antiphons which fall to her choir. The first antiphon of Lauds and Vespers is said after the *Alleluia* or *Laus tibi;* that of Prime, Terce.

Sext, and None, at the end of the *Memento*. She goes to say the versicle of Matins, when *Et in sæcula* of the *Gloria Patri* is said, and afterwards comes to place herself two steps below the Sister who officiates, to say the first Lesson. At the end of the *Precibus* she says the *Jube*, and remains inclined, until she has received the blessing (which ought to be observed by all those who have Lessons to say), then she begins the lesson, inclining as she says, *Tu autem*, &c. When she has said the versicle of the response, she genuflects with the second chorist, and takes her place, making first the inclination to the Superior.

She goes to say the versicle of Lauds, when *Tu Regis alti janua* of the hymn is said, and the versicle of Vespers at *Sit laus Deo Patri*, &c.

When the chapters of Prime, Terce, Sext, None and Compline are begun, she goes to say the versicles with the ceremonies prescribed for the chanter, observing to place herself above the lectern exactly in the middle.

OF THE SECOND CHORIST.

She intones the antiphons which fall to her at Matins, Lauds, and Vespers only. She says the second lesson at Matins, and leaves for this purpose at the versicle of the response of the first, and comes to place herself near the other chorist; being distant two steps one from the other they genuflect together, as has been said. She remains erect until she says the *Jube*, when she inclines towards the Sister who officiates to receive the blessing. Then she begins her lesson, as it has been said for the first chorist; when she has said the versicle of the response, and the *Gloria Patri* as far as the *Sancto*, she retires, making the ordinary ceremony with the chanter.

OF THOSE WHO OUGHT TO SUPPLY FOR THE ABSENT.

When the Sisters who officiate and the chanters are absent, the oldest professed of each choir, or the nearest Sister (if the others do not observe it), should supply for them, supposing they themselves have no office in the choir.

—In the Novitiate houses, the older Novices may be allowed to practise the Office, by supplying for the chanters and the Sister who offciates.

If it be a chorist who is absent, the first novice of her choir supplies, or a postulant if there be no novice, or else the youngest professed.

The youngest professed should be chorist when there are no novices; for this purpose three are chosen from each choir, and each, for her fortnight, places herself the last in rank.

When the Superior has to officiate and is absent from the choir, or otherwise prevented, the Assistant should replace her.

The Assistant is replaced by the oldest professed who has a voice.

When a chanter or chorist of the Superior is absent, one of the oldest professed should supply for her.

The Assistant's chanters and chorists ought to be replaced by Sisters who are more than three years professed.

Of the Ceremonies of the Office.

WHEN TO KNEEL.

The Sisters remain on their knees as much as it is possible for them during mental prayer, which each makes in her ordinary place, and during the time they prepare themselves for the Office.

At Matins, when *Venite adoremus et procedamus ante Deum.* is said, they all bend the knee together; during the verse *Te ergo* of the *Te Deum*, they kneel down.

At Lauds, during the hymn *O Gloriosa*, excepting in the Paschal time, when it is said standing; at Vespers during the first strophe of the *Ave Maris Stella;* at the end of the *Fidelium* of each Office; during the anthems of the Blessed Virgin, excepting at the times prescribed, when they are said standing. When these anthems are said standing, the Sisters kneel down when the last *Amen* is answered, until they leave the choir.

WHEN THE HANDS SHOULD BE JOINED.

The Sisters ought to keep their hands joined from the beginning of the preparations for the Office until the first *Gloria Patri;* during the anthems of the Blessed Virgin, which are said at the end of the Office, whether they are kneeling or standing, and always whilst they are on their knees, as far as they can do so easily. The rest of the time they keep their arms crossed under their scapulars.

WHEN TO MAKE THE SIGN OF THE CROSS.

At Matins they make the sign of the Cross with the thumb upon the mouth, saying *Domine labia mea aperies;*

at Compline, on the breast, saying *Converte nos;* on themselves in the usual manner, saying *Deus in adjutorium;* at the beginning of the canticles, *Benedictus, Magnificat,* and *Nunc dimittis,* and at the end of the *Credo,* which is said after the Office, and in general when they begin to pray, and when they finish.

When the Sisters should turn towards the Altar.

The Sisters are turned towards the Altar from the beginning of each Office, until the chanter has intoned the first psalm.

During the versicles, chapters, and prayers, and during the *Precibus,* until the blessing of the first lesson is given.

When the *Venite exultemus,* the hymns, and canticles, the *Magnificat, Nunc dimittis,* and *Benedictus* are said, and during the anthem of the Blessed Virgin, which is said after the Office. During the remainder of the Office they turn in choir.

When to Stand and when to be Seated.

They are seated during all the psalms, after they are intoned as far as the mediant, excepting during the *Laudate Dominum omnes gentes,* the *Laudate Dominum de cœlis* of Lauds, and the two first verses of the *Laudate pueri Dominum.* They remain standing when the Superior says a lesson, or the Assistant and other Sisters who supply for her when she is absent; they are seated during the other lessons. When the *Tu autem* is said, they rise to say the response; they also rise when the last word of the last verse is said, to say the *Gloria Patri.* They ought not to sit down until after the first verse of the first psalm of each Hour is said.

At the Office for the Dead they remain seated during all the psalms, excepting the *Laudate Dominum de cœlis* of Lauds.

When Holy Communion is given in the choir during the Office, the Sisters stand, and they do the same at the Elevation, if the grate is open.

WHEN TO INCLINE.

The Sisters remain inclined and turned in choir when they say the *Gloria Patri* as far as the *Sancto*, during the verse *Sit nomen* (Psalm 112), and during the last strophe of the hymns in which the Blessed Trinity is named. When the verse *Sit nomen Domini* occurs in a commemoration, as on the feast of the Holy Name of Jesus, the Sisters incline without turning in choir, and also at *Te ergo quæsumus* in the commemoration of the Precious Blood, and at *Verbum caro factum est* in the Christmas Office.

When they say the verse *Sanctus* and *Tu Rex gloriæ Christe* of the *Te Deum*, as well as the verses, *Benedicamus Patrem* (Cant. Daniel 3). At the words *Sanctum et terribile nomen ejus* (Psalm 110), and *Non nobis, Domine* (Psalm 113), they only make an inclination without rising.

At the beginning of each Hour, when the chanter has begun the first psalm, they all make an inclination together towards the Altar, and turn in choir, excepting at Lauds for the Dead, when they are said after Matins.

At the first prayer of each Office the Sisters remain a little inclined until the *Per omnia*. When the Superior or the Assistant gives the blessing at Compline, they turn in choir and incline to receive it.

In the evening after Matins, when the point of meditation has been read, the Superior rises and gives the blessing, the Sisters without rising incline to receive it; they do the same when the Superior says *Nos cum prole pia*, &c., at the end of the *Ave Maria, filia Dei Patris*.

During the Office, when the Holy Name of Mary occurs, or that of the Saint whose feast is kept, the Sisters make an inclination of the head, and the same when they have intoned anything at the Office.

They do not incline when the *Gloria Patri* is said kneeling, nor when any of the verses at which otherwise they would do so, are said, excepting when the Blessed Trinity is named and the Holy Name of Jesus; if they are seated, they incline without rising.

OF THE ORDER TO BE OBSERVED WHEN THE SUPERIOR OFFICIATES.

The Superior officiates on all first class feasts, as also on the feast of Our Lady Mother of the Good Shepherd, and of the Presentation of Our Lady; on the three days of Tenebræ, at the Office for the Dead, on the feast of All Souls, at the decease of the Sisters, and at the Office which is said for the Bishops, Superiors, Confessors, founders, and benefactors of the house.

When the Superior officiates, it is observed to choose the two chorists from amongst the oldest of the professed Sisters, who are on each choir, if they have good voices, and the Assistant with the oldest in Religion are chanters. When the Superior goes to the middle of the choir to officiate, they accompany her, perform all the ceremonies together, and remain at her side, a step below her, all the time she is there. If the Superior is infirm or aged she may officiate in her place instead of going to the lectern.

On the principal feasts of the year, the chanters and chorists may begin together the psalms and antiphons, if the Superior please, for greater solemnity; in this case they meet before the Superior's stall, the chorists leaving at the *Sicut erat*, the chanters at the last word of the *Gloria Patri*, and placing themselves so as to have two steps between them.

The Superior, going out to officiate, does not make the inclination to the statue of our Lady.

Having begun Matins, she returns to her stall, when the *Alleluia* or *Laus tibi* is said, but the two chanters remain in the middle of the choir, to say together the Invitatory and the *Venite;* having finished it, they begin the hymn (or the psalm if there is no hymn) as far as the mediant, and then they retire, observing the ceremonies said above. The two chanters do not kneel in saying *Venite adoremus*, but incline.

The Superior says, in her stall, *Pater noster* and the versicle *Et ne nos;* when she begins the *Precibus* the two chanters come to the middle of the choir to say the lessons; the first inclines, being a little turned towards the Superior to ask the blessing; after she has received it she rises again and begins her lesson, inclining with the other chanter when she says *Tu autem*. They say the versicle of the response together, after the repetition, the second chanter says *Jube*, inclining as has just been said. At the beginning of the versicle the Superior comes to the middle of the choir, passes between the chanters, and says the *Gloria Patri* with them as far as *Sancto*, after which they all three genuflect. The Superior asks the blessing, like the others, turning a little towards the Assistant, who inclines with the other chanter to give it to her. In the absence of the Assistant, the surveillante, or the oldest professed, blesses the Superior. If the Assistant cannot be chanter, she blesses the Superior from her place. The third lesson being finished, the Superior and two chanters intone the *Te Deum*, then all three genuflect and retire.

When the Superior begins the Hours in her stall, the chanters meet a little above her place, when *Sicut erat* is said, to begin the hymn, or the psalm, if there is no hymn. They do not make the inclination going, but only returning.

At Vespers, they intone the first antiphon and the first psalm as far as the mediant and retire. When the Superior has said the Chapter, the chanters in the middle of the choir begin the *Ave Maris Stella*, retiring after the first strophe is said. They go to say the *Benedicamus Domino* when *Et clamor meus* is said, advancing only two steps above the Superior, leaving a space between themselves and making the ceremonies marked above.

At Compline, they begin the first psalm in the middle of the choir, and incline as usual when the first prayer of each Hour is said, rising at the time directed above. At the end of the antiphon, they meet in the middle of the choir for the Litany, which is said kneeling. The Superior goes to the lectern to say the versicle and prayer, then they return to their places, observing to make the ordinary genuflections altogether.

On these solemn days the chanters take the places nearest to the stall of the Superior, and the chorists next to them. When the chanters cannot exercise their charges the chorists supply for them, and the oldest professed Sisters after these are taken for chorists, as has been said.

When the chorists go to say the versicles, and that the Superior is in the middle of the choir, they do not make the inclination to the statue of our Lady, but to the Superior, or to her who officiates for her, in case she were not in her stall, nor the Assistant in hers.

If it happened that the Superior or Assistant could not officiate on the days marked, the same ceremonies would be observed, with regard to the surveillante or her who should be named to take her place; also in case that neither the one nor the other were in the choir, then the inclinations would be made to her, and she would take the most honourable place, which is the one nearest to the stall of the Superior.

When the Assistant officiates entirely for the Superior, the Office is on the Assistant's choir, and she may commence it without giving the Superior notice should she be absent. If the Assistant cannot officiate for the Superior, she ought not to assist the Sister who does, but she names a chanter in her place.

If the Superior be at Matins, the Sisters remain seated whilst the Assistant says the lesson.

When the Divine Office with nine lessons is said, the ceremonies marked for the Feast of the Heart of Mary are observed. The Sister who officiates does not go to the middle of the choir to say the Absolution and give the Blessing.

On the great feasts it is the custom to light two candles before the statue of the Blessed Virgin, during the singing of the *Te Deum*, and the same on Saturdays during the *Inviolata*. If the Officiant asks the blessing of the Superior at the *Inviolata*, she gives it without rising.

OF THE ORDER TO BE OBSERVED WHEN THE ASSISTANT OFFICIATES.

The Assistant officiates on all second-class feasts (except those of the Apostles), on the second feasts of Easter, Pentecost, and Christmas, and the feast of Saint Francis de Sales.

For chanters of the Assistant, the chorists of the Superior are generally taken, and for chorists the next oldest professed Sisters of each choir; they take the places of the chanters and chorists of the Superior.

The chanters accompany the Assistant to begin Matins in the middle of the choir; they remain there to say the Invitatory, the *Venite*, and intone the hymn, or the psalm if there be no hymn. They go to say the lessons when the Assistant says the *Et ne nos inducas*, and after she has given the first blessing, they all three genuflect and the Assistant retires. When the chanters say the versicle of the second response, she returns to say the third lesson; she inclines with the chanters during the *Gloria Patri;* after having said *Sancto*, they genuflect together, the chanters retire, and the Assistant asks the blessing, which the Superior (or in her absence the Surveillante, or oldest professed) gives her; after having said the lesson she intones the *Te Deum*, genuflects, and retires.

When the Assistant goes to begin Vespers, the chanters go with her and remain to intone the antiphon and the psalm. They do not accompany her at the other Hours. If it happened that she could not officiate on the days marked, the surveillante would supply for her or the oldest professed Sister of her choir, who for this purpose would place herself in the stall nearest to that of the Assistant. When the Assistant officiates the chanters say the Litany at the end of Compline.

OF THE OFFICE OF THE THIRD FEASTS.

On the third feasts of Easter, Pentecost, and Christmas, the same ceremonies for the Office are observed, as said above for the Assistant, except that the Officiant, chanters, and chorists of the week officiate, and the chanters do not accompany the officiant. They go to the middle of the choir to say the Invitatory, and also to intone the first antiphon and the first psalm at Vespers, at the *Sicut erat*, so as to be ready to genuflect with the Sister who officiates, when *Alleluia* is said. The blessing is always given by the Superior to the Sister who officiates on the third feasts of Easter, Pentecost, and Christmas.

THE OFFICE FOR THE DEAD.

The Roman Rite is followed for the Office of the Dead; one, three, or five prayers are always said. At the decease of the Sisters and at the anniversaries only one; *Absolve* or *Deus indulgentiam*.

At the beginning of the month, the three prayers annexed to the Office are said, and if *Absolve* has to be added for any deceased Sisters, *Quæsumus* must be added to make the fifth, ending always with *Fidelium Deus*.

The Office of the Dead for all the Faithful departed and in particular for the Sisters of the Institute, is said on the first free day in the month. By free day is meant a semi-double, a simple, or a Feria, therefore this Office cannot be said on a double, nor during an octave. When there is no free day in the month, the Sisters will say the Office for the Dead in private.

The Office for the Dead is said thus: After the *Benedicamus Domino* at Vespers of our Lady, the first chorist intones the antiphon *Placebo Domine*, and the chanter the psalm *Dilexi*, and thus alternately; the same at Matins. The Sister who officiates goes out to say the prayer of Vespers at the end of the *Magnificat*, she kneels until the versicle *Domine exaudi*, when she rises.

The antiphons are intoned as they are in the Breviary. After the *Benedicamus Domino* at Lauds of the ordinary Office, the first chorist begins the antiphon of the Nocturn for the following day; she goes out at the last verse of the last psalm, to say the versicle before the *Pater*, which the Sister who officiates does not begin aloud as usual, but says all in secret. At the end of the *Pater* the Sister who officiates knocks on her Breviary, and the chorist begins the first lesson, the other chorist and afterwards the chanter go to say theirs, when the versicle of the response is said. The chorist goes to say the versicle at Lauds, when the choir says the last verse of the last psalm, and the Sister who officiates goes out at the end of the *Benedictus*, to say the prayer as has been said for Vespers.

The Altar is draped in black at the services for the burials and anniversaries of the Religious, at the anniversaries of their Lordships the Prelates, at the decease of the Superiors and Confessors of the House, and at the Office for these latter is said the prayer *Deus qui inter Apostolicos*.

REMARKS.

When the death of a Sister is announced, a *De profundis* is said with the prayer *Absolve*, which is said in the plural, if there are several deceased.

During thirty days after the death of a Sister in the House, a *De profundis* with the prayer *Quæsumus* is said; if another Sister dies during the time, it is said in the plural.

When this prayer *Quæsumus* is being said, if news is received of the death of one or more Sisters, the prayer *Absolve* must be added, without, however, finishing the first prayer with *Per Christum Dominum nostrum*.

OBSERVATIONS UPON THE OFFICE.

1. The Assistant ought not to name Sisters to officiate whose voices are discordant or unsteady, or give them a charge in the choir, or even let them sing very loud, lest their discordant voices should be heard. All the other Sisters will in turn, according to their rank of the year, officiate at the Office, except the Superior and Assistant, who will only do so on the days appointed.

The Assistant ought to have much at heart, and to pay special attention, that the Sisters continue to sing the Office and all that is written, as it is in the book of plain chant; following the Gregorian custom, in order that nothing may be changed and nothing introduced, which is contrary to simplicity and ordinary usage.

2. Only the Assistant and those who are named to lead and support the choir, are permitted to change the tone of the Office; this does not prevent the chanters from being able to raise it a little in beginning the psalms to keep up the choir and prevent the tone from falling too low, though the chorists should not do so.

3. The Sisters never dispense themselves from saying the Office but for some great necessity, according to the opinion of the Superior, or by the order of the doctor.

4. If any one through weakness or for any other reason, could not make herself heard in the choir, she should not on this account fail to assist at the Office, in the rank which the Superior appoints for her, but she should recite it in secret unless she preferred saying the verses which fall to her choir.

5. Those who are obliged to go out from the Office, or who remember to have omitted something which precedes what is then being said, ought to follow the choir, especially if their voice is of use, and at the end say what they have omitted.

6. Those who say the Office in private are not obliged to say the final antiphon, excepting after Lauds and Compline. They may also defer Lauds till the morning, and say Matins at night; in this case at the end of the *Te Deum*, they finish with the *Divinum auxilium*. At the end of the other Hours, after the *Fidelium*, it is sufficient to say a *Pater* and *Ave* and the *Divinum auxilium*. When the Office is recited in private no ceremonies are made; it is not necessary to say it so loud as to be able to hear oneself distinctly, it suffices to pronounce it well.

7. Those who have the devotion will do well to say the prayer *Sacro Sanctæ*, with the versicle *Beata viscera*, and a *Pater* and *Ave* after the Office. This prayer, raised by the Church to the rank of a Sacramental, obtains for those who recite it piously, dispositions of charity and contrition, which efface the faults committed through frailty in the recitation of the Office, and remits, at least in part, the penalty due to them.

8. When any Sister cannot assist in the choir when the Office for the Dead or other extra Offices, public prayers,

litanies, and the *Stabat* are said, she is not obliged to recite what she has omitted, nor say the Office nor prayers in private, excepting the Office of the day of decease, and that of the anniversary of the Sisters of each House.

9. It is the custom on Saturday after the evening obedience, to go to the choir to sing the *Inviolata*. The Superior places herself in the middle of the choir, holding a lighted candle, the chanter intones the *Inviolata*, the Sister who officiates says the versicle and prayer, and the Superior reads the *Act of Homage to the Blessed Virgin*.

10. The *Pater* and *Ave*, or the *Pater, Ave*, and *Credo* after the Office are said in Latin. Afterwards the sign of the Cross is made.

11. The Lay Sisters are at liberty to say the little Office of the Most Pure Heart of Mary instead of the *Paters* and *Aves* which are prescribed in the Constitutions, Chapter iii.

12. No litanies can be said or sung publicly in the Church except those of the Blessed Virgin, the Saints, and of the Holy Name of Jesus.

Note.—By special Indult of the Holy See, granted to the Congregation of Our Lady of Charity of the Good Shepherd of Angers (June 27, 1898), the Litany of the Sacred Heart of Jesus may also be said or sung publicly in the church.

PARTICULAR OBSERVATIONS ON THE CEREMONIES OF THE OFFICE.

1. The Sisters take care to foresee and study their extra Offices. They say the Office in a moderate tone, without forcing their voices too much and without *jerks*. In psalmody they must avoid lowering the voice at the mediant, and in taking up the verses, in order not to be obliged to raise it at each psalm.

2. The accent must never fall upon a monosyllable; if one or more come at the end of a verse or mediant, the accentuation must be made on the first word of two or more syllables, which precedes these syllables.

3. In singing, as in psalmody, attention must be paid not to drawl the last syllable of words at the mediant, or

at the end of a verse. On the contrary, the last but one of these words must be accentuated, doubling its length, so as to pronounce the syllables which follow, quickly and slightly.

4. In singing, as in psalmody, all the notes must be well joined together, not disjointed in jerks, which produces a very disagreeable effect.

5. Great care must be taken to keep the same tone as the Sister who officiates, both in taking up the intonations of the Office, answering the prayers, the versicles, and in general all that she intones.

If possible, the Office should be recited on the note *fa* or *fa* sharp, taking *sol* for the *Te Deum, Benedictus*, and *Nunc Dimittis*.

6. In singing the Office the Sisters must be careful not to divide the verses of the psalms, before the mediant and the end; if they are too long, they may breathe slightly at the commas, but without making stops.

7. The pauses of the mediant are of a measure of music or else of the time that would be taken to say *Jesus, Maria, Joseph*, and the distance from verse to verse half a measure of music, or the time it would take to repeat *Jesus, Maria*. The Sisters need not hold their books at the ordinary Office, unless they wish it, except the chanters, chorists of the week, and the Sisters of the Novitiate.

8. In all the ceremonies which the Sisters make two and two, they shall pay attention always to turn inwards towards one another, taking care as much as possible never to turn their backs to the Blessed Sacrament, excepting the chanters and chorists, when they return to their places, and when the Sisters leave the choir. In general, all the Sisters ought to conform to one another, both for the genuflections and inclinations (which they ought to make sufficiently low and very reverently), as well as for sitting down, rising, joining the hands, and all turning together, and at the same time, with the greatest gravity, reverence, and modesty that can be, taking care to be always in a straight line, without advancing or standing back, the one more than the other, and when they incline all should do so equally.

The Sisters ought also to pay particular attention to go out at the same moment, and genuflect together when they go to sing anything at the lectern, and the same when returning to their places. When entering the choir to say the Office, they keep their arms crossed under their scapulars, and are attentive, as much as can be, not to walk during the verses when the choir is inclined.

Of the Sermons.

During sermons the sash of the grate ought to be opened and the curtains drawn back, the Religious sit in their stalls, a little turned towards the preacher; when there are vacant places, the Lay Sisters may take them, or sit on little benches before the stalls, or else place themselves in the middle of the choir, accordingly as the Superior thinks best.

The first time the Preacher salutes them, they incline, to return his salutation.

The points are not read at the evening meditation, when there has been a sermon in the afternoon.

Of Reverence and Tranquillity.

The Sisters observe to move as little as possible whilst they are in the choir; if it is necessary to do so, let it be gently and religiously, taking care always, when they cross the choir, to make the genuflection to the Blessed Sacrament and inclination to the Superior. In case she enters the choir or passes them during Holy Mass, or at another time when they are on their knees, they incline without rising; but during the Office they ought to rise if they are seated, to make an inclination to her, or to the one who holds her place. This is to be understood of the Assistant, but not of the surveillantes or senior Sisters.

On Entering and Leaving the Choir.

Every time the Sisters enter the choir for their devotions, and they leave it, they kiss the ground.

If by negligence any one comes late, after the Office is begun, she should kiss the ground before the Superior.

The places of those who leave the choir during the Office ought not to be taken, unless it be certain that they will not return.

The sign being given to leave the choir, they all kiss the ground together and rise. The two last novices advance a little towards the middle of the choir, and, being a step distant from one another, they make the genuflection to the Blessed Sacrament and the inclination to the Superior as they pass before her stall (or else if the convenience of the place will not allow them to do this, they may first make the inclination to the Superior, from their place, so as not to turn their back to the Blessed Sacrament, then make the genuflection with the ceremonies prescribed above), after which they go out, and the others follow consecutively, whilst those who precede them make the inclination to the Superior. Those who are at the lower end of the choir ought not to advance as far forward as the others to make the genuflection, and this is observed on similar occasions. If the number of the Sisters is unequal, the three last make their ceremonies together.

If any Sisters are obliged to leave the choir during the time of the great silence, they ask permission by approaching the Superior a little and making an inclination.

Those who leave the choir for a short time, do not kiss the ground, nor on re-entering it.—When the Blessed Sacrament is exposed, the Sisters genuflect on both knees.

THE TIMES WHEN THE OFFICE MAY BE ADVANCED OR DELAYED.

Matins are advanced a quarter of an hour or more on the days when the Superior officiates, and that the *Te Deum* and *Benedictus* are sung; three-quarters of an hour, when the Divine Office with nine Lessons is said.

When the Office of the Dead is said, Matins are advanced a quarter and a half quarter of an hour; and the same when the three Nocturns are said, because Lauds are always kept for the morning. When it is said in Lent, Vespers are advanced a short quarter of an hour.

During the octave of Corpus Christi and on other days on which there is Benediction, Compline is advanced a quarter of an hour. In Lent, and on the other Fridays of the year when the *Stabat* is sung, Compline is advanced half a quarter of an hour. The *Stabat* is not sung during the octaves of the feasts which we celebrate, nor on the feasts observed in the dioceses where our convents are established. It ought not either to be said when the Church keeps the feast of a double on the Saturday, because the first Vespers begin on the Friday, and they are more solemn than the second. If a feast occurs on the Friday, this does not prevent the *Stabat* being sung, because, the second Vespers being over, the feast is ended.

The Processions.

On Sundays and feasts after Vespers, should the Superior think well, there is a procession round the cloister, or within the enclosure of the garden, if it can be conveniently done. The following order is always observed.

The oldest in profession of the Lay Sisters, or another whom the Superior may appoint, takes the Cross and places herself in the middle of the choir above the lectern. She holds it raised, so that it may be seen, and, according to the Roman custom, she turns the back of the Crucifix to the procession. The young novices (or, if there are none, the two youngest professed Sisters) take the candlesticks, and place themselves on each side of the Cross; at the same time the two chanters of the procession place themselves above the lectern.

In processions they may sing hymns, Litanies, and may even say the Rosary and other vocal prayers, &c. If the Litanies are sung, they begin them on their knees. The Litany of the Saints, on Saint Mark's day, and the Rogation days, being of penance, is begun and ended kneeling.

When the words *Sancta Maria* are said, the procession sets out; the Sisters walk two and two. Those who carry the Cross and candlestcks leave without genuflecting; the bell is rung, and continues to ring until the procession has passed out (and the same when returning as the Cross re-enters the choir). The Lay Sisters and Novices go first, then the Professed, all walking two and two, with an equal and steady step, leaving between them a space of two steps every way; the two chanters walk in the middle of the ranks, to be heard better. The Superior goes alone, the last, if the number of the professed Sisters is unequal, otherwise the Assistant places herself on her left. They do not take holy water, either on leaving or re-entering the choir, but they make an inclination to the statue of the Blessed Virgin, in going out, even if the Superior should not be in her stall.

They may stop in passing before the altar in the cloister, to sing an anthem, or the *Monstra te*, in honour of the Blessed Virgin. The Sisters kneel down when they re-enter the choir. The Superior begins the *Memorare*, or another prayer, which the choir continues; they then retire.

When a procession prescribed by the Church takes place, as on Palm Sunday, the Rogation days, Saint Mark, &c., there should be no other the same day.

The Sisters ought to carry a processional Cross without a veil, at all processions, excepting in Passiontide, when a purple one is used.

At the beginning of the year, the Assistant names two Sisters of those who have the best voices, to be chanters at the processions, and two others to support the choir, who walk two or three ranks lower than the chanters.

The Ceremonies and Order which must be Observed when Holy Mass is Sung.

When the Community is sufficiently numerous, Mass is sung every Sunday and feast of precept, and on those which may be of particular devotion in the Congregation, as also at burials, solemn services for the dead, and on similar occasions which may occur in the course of the year.

Whenever Mass is sung, mantles are worn.

On the principal feasts of the Congregation, there should be a deacon and subdeacon, if possible.

When the Celebrant, with his ministers, at the foot of the altar, commences the psalm *Judica me Deus*, the chanters intone the *Introit*. The Sisters remain kneeling till the priest goes up to the altar, then they rise and remain standing till the *Kyrie;* during the *Kyrie*, they sit down when the Celebrant does so.

They stand while the *Gloria* is intoned and recited by the Celebrant, then sit down until *Cum Sancto Spiritu*.

At *Dominus vobiscum*, and during the prayers, the Sisters stand. During the *Epistle, Gradual, Alleluia*, or *Tract*, all are seated. At the Mass of the Holy Ghost, one of the versicles being *Veni Sancte Spiritus*, they kneel.

During the *Gospel* they stand, sitting down when the Celebrant does so, after having said the *Credo*. At the *Incarnatus est*, they incline without rising, except on the feasts of Christmas and the Annunciation, when they ought to kneel. They rise at the last words of the *Credo, Et vitam*. After *Dominus vobiscum* and *Oremus*, they sit down till the *Preface*, except during the incensing. The Sisters should not fail to rise when the thurifer comes to incense them.

During the *Preface* the Sisters stand till after the *Sanctus*, then kneel until the *Per omnia*, when they rise and remain standing until the priest's *Communion*, during which they kneel.[1]

They sit down as soon as the Celebrant has communicated, only rising at the *Post-Communion*, and remaining standing until the end of Mass, except at the *Blessing*, when they ought to be on their knees.

At Masses for the Dead, the ferias of Advent and Lent, Vigils and Ember Days (except the Vigils of Christmas, the Epiphany, and Pentecost), during the Collects and prayers at the end of Mass, they kneel instead of standing ; also after the *Elevation*, until the *Communion* inclusively.

At the prayers which precede the prophecies on Good

---

[1] In some dioceses they stand after the *Elevation* until the *Post Communion ;* they may, if they prefer it, conform to this practice.

Friday and Holy Saturday, they stand, only genuflecting at *Flectamus genua.*

The *Kyrie, Gloria, Credo, Sanctus,* and *Agnus Dei* are sung alternately from choir to choir, as well as the *Tract,* unless it is a harmonized Mass.

On first and second-class feasts, Sundays during octaves, and when the Blessed Sacrament is exposed, the Sisters may sing at the *Elevation,* the *O Salutaris hostia,* or another liturgical motett. At Masses for the Dead, *Pie Jesu Domine dona eis requiem* is sung three times, and at the last they add *Sempiternam.*

When the Celebrant says *Dominus vobiscum,* or anything else to which they ought to answer, the Sisters must be attentive to d ⟩ so altogether, and in the tone which he has taken.

They make the sign of the Cross at the beginning of Mass, at the end of the *Gloria in excelsis,* saying *Cum Sancto Spiritu;* at the end of the *Credo,* saying, *Et vitam venturi,* and at the end of the *Sanctus,* saying, *Benedictus qui venit.*

They make an inclination without rising when saying *Jesu Christe.* They bow the head at the words: *Adoramus te—Gratias agimus tibi—Suscipe deprecationem nostram* of the *Gloria,* and at the *Credo,* saying: *Simul adoratur;* also at these words, *Gratias agamus Domino Deo nostro* before the *Preface,* and in saying *Oro supplex* of the prose in the Mass for the Dead. They always make an inclination to the Blessed Sacrament before turning in choir.

They turn to the Altar for the prayers, the *Gospel,* the *Preface,* the *Pater,* and *Post-Communion;* they turn in choir during the *Introit, Sanctus,* and *Agnus Dei.*

During the *Libera,* the Sisters stand in choir.

It is the duty of the Assistant to have the singing for Mass practised on Saturdays and the eves of feasts, as well as the commemorations for feasts and Sundays, and for processions and extra Offices.

Ceremonies for Low Mass.

The Sisters make the sign of the Cross at the beginning of Mass, and when the priest says the *Indulgentiam;* at the *Gospel* when he says *Sequentia,* &c., they make a little sign of the Cross with the thumb on the forehead, mouth, and breast; then they incline at the *Laus tibi Domine.*

They incline when saying *Mea culpa* in the *Confiteor,* and during the *Indulgentiam;* when the *Et homo factus est* of the *Credo* is said, if they hear it; at the *Elevation* of the Blessed Sacrament; when they say, *Domine non sum dignus;* and at the end of Mass to receive the Blessing.

They strike their breast, saying *Mea culpa,* in the *Confiteor;* when the *Agnus Dei* is said (except at Masses for the Dead), and at the *Domine, non sum dignus,* which they all say in a low voice, as well as the *Confiteor,* with her who recites it aloud, even when they only communicate spiritually. They kiss the ground when the priest says *Et verbum caro factum est* of the Gospel of St. John, that is said at the end of Mass, which they omit if it is another Gospel.

The Kiss of Peace.

When the Sisters give one another the Kiss of Peace on the days appointed, they do it in this manner: at the end of Mass the Superior gives the sign, each one rises and remains standing in her place, turned in choir. The *Laudate* is intoned.

The Assistant receives the Kiss of Peace from the Superior kneeling, making her an inclination before and after; then she gives it to the Sister who is nearest to her, and thus consecutively they give it to one another.

The second Assistant in the Mother House (and in the foundations, the chanter of the other choir) also receives it from the Superior, doing the same as has been said for the Assistant. All observe to make one another an inclination before and afterwards. In giving it, the first says: *My Sister, pray to God for me,* the other replies: *My Sister,*

God give us His peace; but to the Superior they say: *My Mother, pray to God for me,* and she answers: *My daughter, I receive you in peace.*

THE BELLS, AND OF THE ORDER TO BE OBSERVED IN RINGING THE BELLS FOR THE OFFICE AND EXERCISES OF THE CONVENT.

There should be two principal bells; the Church, or large bell, the weight of which should be in proportion to the size of the Convents, or according to their means; and the Convent bell, to ring for the Exercises, ought to be of less weight than the former.

The gate bell ought to be large enough to be easily heard; besides these, there should be one at the *Turn*, to call the Sister Tourières; one in the Sacristy, which serves for those within and without, to summon the Sister Sacristan.

There should be, if possible, a clock and an alarum, which the Lay Sisters wind up in the evening, setting it for half-past four in summer and five in winter, in order that at the right time they may give the sign with the *crécelle* for the Sisters to rise.

The morning *Angelus* is rung on the Church bell, a little after the sign for rising; as also that of noon, and of the evening, nine strokes at three times, distant an *Ave Maria* from one another, and afterwards a peal is rung for the space of a *Pater*. On Chapter days, if it be held in the afternoon, ten or twelve strokes are tolled after the *Angelus*, and if it be in the morning, as many are tolled before holding it.

For the morning's meditation, one hundred and eighty strokes are tolled.

All the Offices are rung for the space of a *Pater* and *Ave* (on the great solemnities of the year they may be rung a rather longer time), and at the last peal for Vespers and Matins, five or six strokes are tolled at the end. On the principal feasts of the year, the bell is rung during the *Te Deum* at Matins.

The bell is rung for the Community Mass during the space of a *Pater* and *Ave*, tolling twelve strokes at the end. When the Priest begins the *Preface*, the bell is rung, tolling three times nine strokes, at a little distance from one another, and slowly, so that the last nine strokes may finish, if it can be, with the *Sanctus*. The other Masses are rung for in the same way, except that no bell is rung at the *Preface*, and that for those which are said before that of the Community, five strokes are tolled first.

For **High Mass**, the bell is rung at the second psalm of Sext until the anthem, tolling afterwards forty or fifty strokes until the end of the prayer. At the end of None thirty or forty strokes are again rung.

For **Sermons** the bell is tolled during the *Magnificat*, more or less, according to the custom of the place.

During Lent, and on the Fridays of the year on which the *Stabat* is sung, two strokes are rung at the beginning of the anthem, which is said at the end of Compline. Every day four strokes are tolled at twice, at the beginning of the Litany, for the meditation, which is also done on Sundays and feasts, half an hour before the Spiritual Reading.

To assemble the Sisters in the choir, five strokes are rung slowly on the Church bell; and to call them to the extraordinary Chapter, seven strokes.

For the Office of the Dead, at the beginning of the month, the bell should be rung at the *Magnificat*, and at the *Benedictus* of the Office of the Blessed Virgin.

When the Holy Communion is taken to the sick, eight strokes are tolled to assemble the Community.

For Extreme Unction, six strokes are rung to assemble the Community in the Infirmary.

When the sick person enters her agony, fifteen strokes at three times are rung, each at the distance of a *Pater* and *Ave*, leaving between each stroke the space of an *Ave*; for the decease, six strokes at three times; each of these three interruptions ought to last the time of a *Requiem*, and afterwards thirty strokes are tolled, leaving between each the space of a *Requiem*.

The Convent bell is rung five or seven minutes before Terce, Vespers, and Compline, to assemble the Sisters. On the shortest days in winter, the *Angelus* may serve for the signal for Compline, and as soon as the Convent bell has rung, the Sisters go straight into the choir to say it. On the longest days in summer, the *Angelus* may serve for the first or last bell for Matins.

To assemble the Community in the Refectory, the Convent bell is rung twice for the space of a *Pater*, leaving a quarter of an hour between each peal, and at the end of the last, they toll four or five strokes. At the end of the first table, a short volley is rung for the second.

Half a quarter of an hour before the hour of silence, the signal for the Obedience is given, and that of the afternoon silence is rung on the same bell.

The Convent bell is also rung at the beginning and end of the Spiritual Reading; a peal is rung on the same bell for Confessions, adding five or six strokes at the end. This bell is rung when the morning silence on fasting days begins.

Remark.—On other occasions when bells ought to be rung, the custom of the diocese is followed; if convenience or particular circumstances require it, even the above rules may be modified.

INTENTIONS FOR THE CUSTOMARY PRAYERS.

Before Prime (or after Mass).

Ave Maria for the conversion of sinners.
Laudate in thanksgiving for the Generalate.
De profundis for the deceased Sisters.

After Prime.

Ave Maria, Filia Dei Patris for the conversion of the penitents.
Memorare for the Superior General.
Sancta Trinitas unus Deus, miserere nobis.

Monstra te, to place the Community under the protection of the Blessed Virgin.

Omnes Sancti et Sanctæ Dei, intercedite pro nobis.

After Obedience.

Veni Sancte, to obtain good vocations.

Memorare, that there may never be a bad Religious in the Congregation.

Ave Cor Sanctissimum, for the particular needs of the Institute.

O my loving Jesus, in honour of the Sacred Heart of Jesus.

After Matins.

Ave Maria for Benefactors.

Ave Cor Sanctissimum, to ask for union among the houses of the Institute.

Veni Sancte Spiritus, to implore the light of the Holy Ghost.

Three times, *A subitanea et improvisa morte*, to obtain a good death.

On Wednesday, after Mass, the Superior says the *Prayer to Saint Joseph*, with a *Pater* and *Ave*, and three times the invocation, *Saint Joseph, pray for us*.

On Friday, she makes an *Act of Reparation* to the Sacred Heart of Jesus.

On Saturday, before Matins, the *Inviolata*, with the *Act of Homage* to the Blessed Virgin, in reparation for the faults of the week.

The *De profundis* after meals is said for deceased Benefactors.

On the feasts of our Lord and the Blessed Virgin, the Community must not fail to say, in public, the prayers specified at the end of our Spiritual Exercises.

RECOMMENDATIONS TO WHICH ALL THE HOUSES SHOULD CONFORM.

The above prayers ought to be said in all the houses of the Congregation, and for the same intentions. In order not to burden the Community, and to preserve the uniformity which ought to reign in every part of the Institute, others cannot be substituted or added.

Special devotions, however, may be made during the months consecrated to the Sacred Heart of Jesus, the Blessed Virgin and Saint Joseph, as well as novenas at times of public calamities and other necessities, or to comply with the request of persons who recommend themselves to the prayers of the Religious; but these prayers and novenas must only be made for a definite time, and must never be introduced into the customs of any Community by a Superior.

PRAYERS WHICH ARE SAID WHEN THE BISHOP OR THE ECCLESIASTICAL SUPERIOR MAKES THE CANONICAL VISITATION OF THE CONVENT.

The Prelate, having entered the choir of the Religious, with the ceremonies prescribed in the Book of Customs, says the following prayers, to which the Sisters answer:

V. Adjutorium nostrum in nomine Domini.
R. Qui fecit cœlum et terram.
V. Sit nomen Domini benedictum.
R. Ex hoc nunc et usque in sæculum.
V. Emitte Spiritum tuum et creabuntur.
R. Et renovabis faciem terræ.
V. Memento, Domine, in beneplacito populi tui.
R. Visita nos in salutari tuo.
V. Domine, exaudi orationem meam.
R. Et clamor meus ad te veniat.
V. Dominus vobiscum.
R. Et cum spiritu tuo.

Oremus.

Conscientias nostras, quæsumus, Domine, visitando purifica, ut veniens Dominus Jesus Christus, paratam sibi in nobis inveniat mansionem.

Adesto supplicationibus nostris, Omnipotens Deus, et quibus fiduciam sperandæ pietatis indulges, intercedente beato Patre Augustino, confessore tuo atque pontifice, consuetæ misericordiæ tuæ tribue benignus effectum. Per Dominum nostrum, &c.

R. Amèn.

Then he gives the blessing.

PRAYERS WHICH ARE SAID IN THE CHAPTER.

The Community, being assembled in Chapter, and the Prelate, in the place which has been prepared for him, begins the *Veni Sancte Spiritus*, which the Sisters continue.

The Prelate says:

V. Emitte Spiritum tuum et creabuntur.
R. Et renovabis faciem terræ.

Oremus.

Deus, qui corda fidelium Sancti Spiritus illustratione docuisti, da nobis in eodem Spiritu recta sapere, et de ejus semper consolatione gaudere. Per Christum Dominum nostrum.

R. Amen.

The Prelate then makes his exhortation, after which he says:

Ecce ab ostio, venio Dominus Deus vester, visitare vos in pace.

V. Adjutorium nostrum in nomine Domini.
R. Qui fecit cœlum et terram.

And the rest as above.

Oremus.

Deus qui corda fidelium, &c.

Aurem tuam, quæsumus, Domine, precibus nostris accommoda, et mentis nostræ tenebras gratia tuæ visitationis illustra. Qui vivis et regnas, &c.

Oremus.

Conscientias nostras, &c., as above.

Generalis absolutio.

Per meritum Passionis et Resurrectionis Domini nostri Jesu Christi; per intercessionem beatæ Mariæ semper Virginis et omnium Sanctorum, misereatur vestri, omnipotens Deus, et dimittat vobis omnia peccata vestra et perducat vos ad vitam æternam.
R. Amen.

Extending his right hand over them, he says:

Dominus noster Jesus Christus, qui dixit discipulis suis, quæcumque ligaveritis super terram, erunt ligata et in cœlis, et quæcumque solveritis super terram, erunt soluta et in cœlis ; de quorum numero me indignum et peccatorum ministrum esse voluit ; intercedente gloriosissima semperque Virgine ipsius Genitrice Maria, beato Michaele archangelo, et beato Petro Apostolo, cui data es potestas ligandi et absolvendi, et omnibus Sanctis, ipse vos, per ministerium nostrum absolvat ab omnibus peccatis vestris, quæcumque cogitatione, aut locutione, aut operatione, seu omissione et negligentia egistis, atque ab eorum vinculis absolutas perducere dignetur ad regna cœlorum. Qui cum Patre et Spiritu Sancto vivit et regnat, &c. Benedictio Domini nostri Jesu Christi descendat super vos et maneat semper. In nomine Patris †, et Filii, et Spiritus Sancti.
R. Amen.

After the prayers the Sisters retire two and two, without any other sign, excepting the Sister whom the Superior wishes to remain with her to accompany the Prelate or other Superior.

THE ORDER WHICH MUST BE OBSERVED WHEN THE BISHOP COMES TO THE CONVENT TO ADMINISTER THE SACRAMENT OF CONFIRMATION.

The Sacristan shall prepare what is necessary, having a little table placed in the exterior Church, covered with a cloth, on which there should be a basin and jug, with a towel over it, and some crumb of bread on a plate. She shall also have a *prie-dieu* placed before the altar and a chair before the grate.

A little before his Lordship arrives, twelve strokes are rung on the great bell to assemble the Community. All the Religious take their places, kneeling in the choir.

The Boarders and other inmates of the house who are to be confirmed, shall be kneeling in order before the grate, with their hands joined.

If Mass is said, they hear it with the grate open, after which, the Bishop comes forward, and when he pronounces the words, *Spiritus Sanctus superveniat in vos*, all the Religious rise and stand turned towards the altar.

The prayers being said, the Religious place themselves on their knees, and remain kneeling whilst the Bishop gives Confirmation.

The Superior, standing close to the grate on the right side, presents those who are to be confirmed one after the other, making them kneel down on the step of the grate; the Assistant or the Mistress directs them to retire on the other side.

A Priest says the names in Latin to the Bishop, but the children ought always to have them written on a piece of paper which they hold in their hand.

The Prelate having finished Confirmation, and given Benediction, the Community retires.

In dioceses where it is the custom to put a band over the forehead, those who have been confirmed wear it all day.

The Order which must be Observed when a Secular makes her Profession of Faith.

If it should happen that any Boarder desiring to become a Catholic, wishes to be instructed in the Convent, not having as yet made her abjuration, on the day appointed for the ceremony, when the Bishop (or his delegate) has arrived, she shall leave the enclosure and be placed in the hands of her relations, or other well-known persons, who will conduct her to the exterior Church, where she shall make her profession of faith; meanwhile, the grate of the choir shall be open, and the Religious shall place themselves near it on their knees.

If any among the penitents wish to be received into the Church, the Superior will cause them to go outside, to make their abjuration, if she thinks well, or she will permit them to make it in their choir, in the hands of a Priest deputed for this purpose.

TABLE INDICATING THE HOURS AT WHICH MATINS MAY BE ADVANCED FOR THE NEXT DAY.

Grave reason is required to change the hour for Matins; this necessity can only present itself rarely for the whole Community.

When, on account of illness or other reasons, the Sisters are obliged to say Matins in private, they cannot do so before the hours named below.

20 January	at a quarter-past two.
13 February	at half-past two.
1 March	at a quarter to three.
18 March	at three o'clock.
4 April	at a quarter-past three.
20 April	at half-past three.
10 May	at a quarter to four.
8 June	at four o'clock.
30 July	at a quarter to four.
21 August	at half-past three.
7 September	at a quarter-past three.
25 September	at three o'clock.
13 October	at a quarter to three.
20 October	at half-past two.
18 November	at a quarter-past two.
15 December	at two o'clock.

Ceremonial of the Last Sacraments.

THE ORDER WHICH MUST BE OBSERVED WHEN THE HOLY SACRAMENTS ARE ADMINISTERED TO THE SICK.

When it is necessary to give the Holy Sacraments to the sick, the utmost reverence shall be observed.

The altar of the infirmary should be prepared as neatly as can be, a crucifix shall be placed on it, two lighted wax candles, a corporal, a little glass with water for the Priest to purify his fingers, a purificator to wipe them, and holy water at the side of the altar.

The stole shall be white when the Priest carries the Blessed Sacrament, purple for Extreme Unction.

Holy Communion.

When the Holy Communion is to be taken to the sick, eight strokes are tolled slowly to assemble the Sisters in the choir, where they ought to go promptly, placing themselves on their knees in a straight line before the step of their stalls, the novices and Lay Sisters at the lower end of the choir, or ante-choir, as convenient, so that they may leave sufficient space for the Priest to pass with the Blessed Sacrament.[1]

Before the Priest takes the holy Ciborium out of the Tabernacle, the Sister Sacristan opens the grate of the choir, and she (or the acolyte) goes before the Priest, ringing a

---

[1] For Communions of devotion all the Sisters are not obliged to accompany the Blessed Sacrament; six, or even four, Sisters suffice.

little bell, and two Sisters carry lighted candles before the Blessed Sacrament.

The Novices and Lay Sisters walk first, and arrange themselves near the infirmary. The Superior, Assistant, and two surveillantes follow next after the Blessed Sacrament, having each a lighted wax candle; the other professed Sisters follow according to their rank of the year, beginning with the last. In the absence of the Assistant and the surveillantes, the oldest professed Sisters carry the candles. The four who carry the candles say with the Priest the alternate verses of the Psalm *Miserere;* and the rest of the Religious say the others, in a low and solemn voice.

Psalm L.

Miserere mei, Deus, secundum magnam misericordiam tuam.

Et secundum multitudinem miserationum tuarum, dele iniquitatem meam.

Amplius lava me ab iniquitate mea: et a peccato meo munda me.

Quoniam iniquitatem meam ego cognosco: et peccatum meum contra me est semper.

Tibi soli peccavi, et malum coram te feci: ut justificeris in sermonibus tuis, et vincas cum judicaris.

Ecce enim in iniquitatibus conceptus sum: et in peccatis concepit me mater mea.

Ecce enim veritatem dilexisti: incerta et occulta sapientiæ tuæ manifestasti mihi.

Asperges me hyssopo, et mundabor: lavabis me, et super nivem dealbabor.

Auditui meo dabis gaudium et lætitiam: et exultabunt ossa humiliata.

Averte faciem tuam a peccatis meis: et omnes iniquitates meas dele.

Cor mundum crea in me Deus: et spiritum rectum innova in visceribus meis.

Ne projicias me a facie tua: et spiritum sanctum tuum ne auferas a me.

Redde mihi lætitiam salutaris tui: et spiritu principali confirma me.

Docebo iniquos vias tuas: et impii ad te convertentur.

Libera me de sanguinibus Deus, Deus salutis meæ: et exultabit lingua mea justitiam tuam.

Domine, labia mea aperies: et os meum annuntiabit laudem tuam.

Quoniam si voluisses sacrificium, dedissem utique: holocaustis non delectaberis.

Sacrificium Deo spiritus contribulatus: cor contritum et humiliatum, Deus, non despicies.

Benigne fac, Domine, in bona voluntate tua Sion: ut ædificentur muri Jerusalem.

Tunc acceptabis sacrificium justitiæ oblationes, et holocausta: tunc imponent super altare tuum vitulos.

Gloria Patri, &c.

On entering the infirmary, those who carry the candles place themselves three or four steps from the bed of the sick person, and the other Religious farther off, all being on their knees, turned towards the Blessed Sacrament. If the heat were great, the room so small that the sick person would be inconvenienced, or that the illness were infectious, only those should enter whom the Mother Superior shall have appointed.

The Priest having reached the infirmary, whether he has finished the psalm or not, says aloud: *Pax huic domui.* The Sisters answer: *Et omnibus habitantibus in ea*, which is observed every time the priest enters the infirmary. The Priest places the holy Ciborium upon the altar, before which he remains kneeling, until the Religious have entered; then rising, he gives holy water to the sick, and sprinkles those who are assisting, saying the antiphon, *Asperges me*, &c., and the first verse of the Psalm *Miserere*, &c., *Gloria Patri*, &c., *Sicut erat*, &c., repeats the antiphon, *Asperges me*, &c., genuflects, and, turning to the Blessed Sacrament, he says:

V. Adjutorium nostrum † in nomine Domini.
R. Qui fecit cœlum et terram.
V. Domine, exaudi orationem meam.
R. Et clamor meus ad te veniat.

V. Dominus vobiscum.
R. Et cum spiritu tuo.

Oremus.

Exaudi nos, Domine sancte, Pater omnipotens, æterne Deus, et mittere digneris sanctum Angelum tuum de cœlis, qui custodiat, foveat, protegat, visitet atque defendat omnes habitantes in hoc habitaculo. Per Christum Dominum nostrum.
R. Amen.

If the sick Sister communicate as Viaticum, she asks pardon of the Superior and of the Community in general, for the causes of pain and disedification which she has given them, begging them to pray for her; the Superior answers the sick Sister in the name of all, that they not only forgive her, but they beg her also to forgive them.

All Religious who, at the hour of death, being contrite and having confessed and communicated, or who, not being able to communicate, shall invoke the Holy Name of Jesus, in their hearts, if they cannot pronounce it with their lips, gain a Plenary Indulgence.

This Indulgence is gained without either cross or medal, but only by reason of the religious profession.

The Superior or the Assistant says the *Confiteor*. The Priest, a little turned towards the sick person, says the *Misereatur* and *Indulgentiam*. After having genuflected, he takes the Blessed Sacrament, and, holding It raised above the holy Ciborium, turned towards the sick person, he says: *Ecce Agnus Dei*, &c., and three times: *Domine non sum dignus*, &c., which she shall endeavour to say in secret. He communicates her, saying: *Accipe, soror, viaticum corporis Domini nostri Jesu Christi, qui te custodiat ab hoste maligno, et perducat te ad vitam æternam. Amen.*

If the sick person has difficulty in swallowing the Sacred Host, a little wine and water may be given her; if any remain, it shall be thrown into the fire, with the ablution of the Priest.

When the Sister is in danger of death, the Priest

receives the renewal of her vows before communicating her, with the same formula as on the feast of the Presentation.

The Priest having replaced the holy Ciborium on the altar, genuflects, washes his fingers, and wipes them on the purificator; then, turned towards the Blessed Sacrament, he says:

V. Dominus vobiscum.
R. Et cum spiritu tuo.

Oremus.

Domine sancte, Pater omnipotens, æterne Deus, te fideliter deprecamur, ut accipienti sorori nostræ sacrosanctum corpus Domini nostri Jesu Christi Filii tui, tam corpori quam animæ prosit ad remedium sempiternum. Qui tecum vivit et regnat in unitate Spiritus Sancti Deus; per omnia sæcula sæculorum.
R. Amen.

The prayer being finished, the Priest may briefly exhort the sick person to thanksgiving for so great a benefit; then he genuflects, blesses her with the holy Ciborium without saying anything, and begins the Psalm *Laudate Dominum de cœlis*, or the *Te Deum*, according to the custom of the place.

The Religious kneel, forming two choirs until the Blessed Sacrament has passed; then they rise and return in the same order in which they came. Having reached the church, they place themselves on their knees before their stalls; the Priest places the holy Ciborium upon the altar, saying the antiphon, *O Sacrum convivium*, and the V. *Panem de cœlo*, &c., with the prayer, *Deus qui nobis, sub sacramento*, &c., at the end of which he gives the blessing in silence, and puts away the Blessed Sacrament; the candles are extinguished immediately, and after the sign all retire.

Extreme Unction.

When it is necessary to administer the Sacrament of Extreme Unction to the sick, the Sister Sacristan tolls six strokes slowly, to assemble the Sisters in the infirmary, where they place themselves on their knees. Before the Priest brings the Holy Oils, the infirmarian ought to have a Ritual ready for his use, and all else necessary for the administration of the Sacrament, as is explained in her *Directory*.

The Priest, in a surplice and purple stole, takes the Holy Oils (which ought to be in a silver case and locked up in the Sacristy, not in the Tabernacle), the Assistant and one of the surveillantes or portresses go to meet him at the enclosure door to conduct him to the infirmary. On entering, he says *Pax huic domui*. The acolyte answers: *Et omnibus habitantibus in eâ*. He places the case containing the Holy Oils upon the altar, sprinkles the sick person with holy water, in the form of a cross, and all who are present, saying the antiphon, *Asperges me*, with the first verse of the Psalm *Miserere*, the *Gloria Patri*, &c., *Sicut erat*, &c., and repeats the antiphon, *Asperges me*, &c.

When the Priest begins the anointing, the Sisters say the *Miserere*.

Pious Reflections for Extreme Unction.

At the Anointing of the Eyes.

The sick Sister should resign herself to the loss of sight by death, in atonement for having used it to look at vain and forbidden objects, or in shedding useless tears. To ask pardon of God for this, to wish to make use of her sight only to see Jesus Christ in Paradise, begging of Him to cast on her those loving looks which He cast on those who crucified Him, or to apply to her soul the tears He shed for our salvation.

"Who will give water to my head, and a fountain of tears to my eyes, and I will weep day and night." (Jerem.

9, 1.) " I have lifted up my eyes to thee who dwellest in Heaven." (Psalm 122, 1.)

At the Anointing of the Ears.

To accept the privation of the sense of hearing in atonement for having listened to evil words and taken pleasure in such; asking pardon of God, and desiring during the time that remains to listen only to words conducive to salvation; asking of Jesus Christ the application of the merit of His patience in listening to the insults and blasphemies of His Passion. " Make me hear Thy voice, O Lord, for Thy voice is sweet." (Cant.)

At the Anointing of the Nostrils.

To ask pardon of God for the sins committed by the sense of smell, and especially for having been, by disedifying conduct, a bad odour to one's neighbour; to offer, in satisfaction to His justice, the corruption of the body, asking of Jesus Christ the application of the merits of the offensive odours He was pleased to endure in the stable and on Mount Calvary.

" Receive, O Lord, my life, my heart, and my body, as an odour of sweetness."

At the Anointing of the Mouth.

To accept the silence of death to satisfy the justice of God in punishment of all the sins committed by the tongue, and the indulgence of the appetite; to receive the anointing, imploring the divine mercy, with a truly humble heart, and asking of Jesus Christ the application of the merits of His silence, His preaching, and His holy fasts.

" If I would justify myself, my own mouth shall condemn me." (Job 9, 20.)

At the Anointing of the Hands.

To be willing that these hands become useless, in punishment of the faults committed by the touch, by injustice, and by the omission of good which ought to have been done; asking pardon for this of God and begging of Jesus Christ the application of the merits of the holy actions He performed with His sacred hands, which were afterwards fastened to the Cross.

" I will wash my hands in Thy name."

At the Anointing of the Feet.

To accept, in satisfaction to the justice of God, that the feet shall be hidden in the grave in penance for having wandered from Him, and to ask of Jesus Christ the application of the merits of so many steps which He took for the salvation of men, especially whilst carrying His Cross.

" I have gone astray like a sheep that was lost; seek thy servant." (Psalm 118.)

" Lead me into the paths of Thy commandments." (Psalm 118.)

The anointing finished, the Priest washes his hands, rubbing them with the crumb of bread, which must be afterwards burnt, as also the little balls of wool which have been used to wipe off the Holy Oil, the ashes of which should be thrown into the piscina. (If the piscina were deep enough, the bread and cotton wool ought to be thrown into it without burning them.) Afterwards he begins the following prayers:

V. Kyrie, &c.   R. Christe, &c.
V. Kyrie, &c.   Pater noster, &c., *in secret*.
V. Et ne nos inducas in tentationem.
R. Sed libera nos a malo.
V. Salvam fac ancillam tuam.
R. Deus meus, sperantem in te.
V. Mitte ei, Domine, auxilium de sancto.
R. Et de Sion tuere eam.
V. Esto ei, Domine, turris fortudinis.
R. A facie inimici.
V. Nihil proficiat inimicus in ea.
R. Et filius iniquitatis non apponat nocere ei.

V. Domine, exaudi orationem meam.
R. Et clamor meus ad te veniat.
V. Dominus vobiscum.
R. Et cum spiritu tuo.

Oremus.

Domine Deus omnipotens, qui per Apostolum tuum Jacobum locutus es, dicens: " Infirmatur quis in vobis, inducat presbyteros ecclesiæ, et orent super eum, ungentes eum oleo in nomine Domini, et oratio fidei salvabit infirmum, et alleviabit eum Dominus, et si in peccatis sit, remittentur ei:" cura quæsumus, Redemptor noster, gratia Sancti Spiritus languores istius infirmi, ejusque sana vulnera, et dimitte peccata, atque dolores cunctos mentis et corporis ab eo expelle, plenamque interius et exterius sanitatem misericorditer redde, ut ope misericordiæ tuæ restitutus, ad pristina reparetur officia. Qui cum Patre et Spiritu Sancto vivis et regnas Deus in sæcula sæculorum. Amen.

Let us pray.

Lord God Almighty, who hast spoken by thine Apostle James, saying: " Is any man sick among you? Let him bring in the priests of the Church, and let them pray over him, anointing him with oil in the name of the Lord, and the prayer of faith shall save the sick man; and the Lord shall raise him up: and if he be in sins, they shall be forgiven him:" cure, we beseech thee, O our Redeemer, by the grace of the Holy Spirit, the languors of this thy servant who is sick; heal his wounds, and forgive his sins: drive out from him all pains of body and mind, and mercifully restore to him full health, inwardly and outwardly, that, being recovered by the help of thy mercy, he may return to his former duties. Who, with the Father and the Holy Ghost, livest and reignest God, world without end. Amen.

Oremus.

Respice, quæsumus, Domine, famulum tuum N., infirmitate sui corporis fatiscentem, et animam refove quam creasti: ut castigationibus emendatus, se tua sentiat medicina salvatum.

Let us pray.

Look down, O Lord, we beseech thee, upon thy servant N., fainting in the infirmity of his body, and refresh the soul which thou hast created, that, being amended by chastisements, he may

Per Christum Dominum nostrum. Amen.

Oremus.

Domine sancte, Pater omnipotens, æterne Deus, qui benedictionis tuæ gratiam ægris infundendo corporibus, facturam tuam multiplici pietate custodis : ad invocationem tui nominis benignus assiste, ut famulum tuum ab ægritudine liberatum et sanitate donatum dextera tua erigas, virtute confirmes, potestate tuearis, atque ecclesiæ tuæ sanctæ cum omni desiderata prosperitate restituas. Per Christum Dominum nostrum. Amen.

feel himself saved by thy medicine. Through Christ our Lord. Amen.

Let us pray.

O holy Lord, almighty Father, eternal God, who, by pouring the grace of thy blessing upon sick bodies, dost preserve, by thy manifold goodness, the work of thy hands, graciously draw near at the invocation of thy name, that, delivering thy servant from sickness, and bestowing health upon him, thou mayest raise him up by thy right hand, strengthen him by thy might, defend him by thy power, and restore him to thy holy Church, with all desired prosperity. Through Christ our Lord. Amen.

The Form of conferring the Last Blessing and Plenary Indulgence.

On entering the dying person's room, the Priest says :

V. Pax huic domui.
R. Et omnibus habitantibus in ea.

V. Peace be to this house.
R. And to all who dwell therein.

Then is said the *Asperges*, after which the Priest says :

V. Adjutorium nostrum in nomine Domini.
R. Qui fecit cœlum et terram.

V. Our help is in the name of the Lord.
R. Who hath made heaven and earth.

The Antiphon.

Ne reminiscaris, Domine, delicta famuli tui (*vel* ancillæ

Remember not, O Lord, the offences of thy servant

tuæ), neque vindictam sumas de peccatis ejus.

Kyrie eleison. Christe eleison. Kyrie eleison.

Pater noster, &c.
V. Et ne nos inducas in tentationem.
R. Sed libera nos a malo.

V. Salvum (salvam) fac servum tuum (ancillam tuam).
R. Deus meus, sperantem in te.
V. Domine, exaudi orationem meam.
R. Et clamor meus ad te veniat.
V. Dominus vobiscum.
R. Et cum spiritu tuo.

Oremus.

Clementissime Deus, Pater misericordiarum, et Deus totius consolationis, qui neminem vis perire in te credentem atque sperantem, secundum multitudinem miserationum tuarum respice propitius famulum tuum (famulam tuam) N., quem (quam) tibi vera fides et spes Christiana commendant. Visita eum (eam) in salutari tuo, et per Unigeniti tui passionem et mortem, omnium ei delictorum suorum remissionem et veniam clementer indulge, ut ejus anima in hora exitus sui te judicem propitiatum inveniat, et in sanguine ejusdem Filii tui ab omni macula abluta, transire ad vitam mereatur perpetuam. Per

(*or* thy handmaid), and take not revenge of *his* sins.

Lord have mercy. Christ have mercy. Lord have mercy.

Our Father, &c.
V. And lead us not into temptation.
R. But deliver us from evil.

V. O Lord, save thy servant (thy handmaid).
R. Who hopeth in thee, O my God.
V. O Lord, hear my prayer.
R. And let my cry come unto thee.
V. The Lord be with you.
R. And with thy spirit.

Let us pray.

O most gracious God, Father of mercies and God of all consolation, who wouldst that none should perish who believe and hope in thee; according to the multitude of thy mercies, look favourably upon thy servant N., whom a true Christian faith and hope commend unto thee. Visit *him* in thy salvation; and through the passion and death of thy Only-begotten, graciously grant unto *him* the pardon and remission of all *his* sins, that *his* soul, at the hour of its departure, may find in thee a most merciful judge; and, cleansed from every stain in the blood of the same thy cumdem Christum Dominum nostrum.

Son, may be worthy to pass to everlasting life. Through the same Christ our Lord.

Then the *Confiteor* being repeated by one of the attendant clerks, the Priest says, *Misereatur*, &c., and then proceeds thus:

Dominus noster Jesus Christus Filius Dei vivi, qui beato Petro Apostolo suo dedit potestatem ligandi atque solvendi, per suam piissimam misericordiam recipiat confessionem tuam, et restituat tibi stolam primam, quam in baptismate recepisti; et ego, facultate mihi ab Apostolica Sede tributa, indulgentiam plenarium et remissionem omnium peccatorum tibi concedo. In nomine Patris, et Filii, et Spiritus Sancti.
R. Amen.
Per Sacrosancta humanæ reparationis mysteria, remittat tibi omnipotens Deus præsentis et futuræ vitæ pœnas, paradisi portas aperiat, et ad gaudia sempiterna perducat. Amen.

Benedicat te omnipotens Deus; Pater, et Filius, et Spiritus Sanctus. Amen.

May our Lord Jesus Christ, Son of the Living God, who gave to his blessed Apostle Peter the power of binding and loosing, in his most loving mercy receive thy confession, and restore to thee that first robe which thou didst receive in baptism; and by the faculty given to me by the Apostolic See, I grant to thee a plenary indulgence and remission of all thy sins. In the name of the Father, and of the Son, and of the Holy Ghost.
R. Amen.
Through the most sacred mysteries of man's redemption, may God almighty remit to thee the pains of the present and the future life, open to thee the gates of Paradise, and bring thee to everlasting joys. Amen.

May God almighty bless thee; Father, and Son, and Holy Ghost. Amen.

Order of the Recommendation of the Soul.

When it is thought that the sick person is entering her agony, the Priest is asked to return (if he be absent), to assist her, and say the prayers for the agonizing.—See the Roman Ritual, which ought to be in each infirmary, unless it is wished to make the recommendation of the soul in the vernacular.—The Sister Sacristan shall ring five strokes on the church bell to give notice to the Sisters to go to the infirmary, in order to unite their prayers to those of the Priest, and to pay the last duties to their Sister.

Care shall be taken to recommend her to the prayers of the neighbouring Convents, according to the custom of the place; the note shall be written in this manner:

"Rev. ———, You are very humbly asked by the Religious of Our Lady of Charity of the Good Shepherd to recommend to God, in your holy prayers, one of their dear Sisters at the point of death in their house of ...... day ...... of the ...... month of ...... year ...."

The Agony.

When the prayers for the agonizing are begun, the Sister Sacristan rings fifteen strokes at three times, leaving between each five the space of a *Pater* and *Ave*, and between each stroke that of half an *Ave*. This is not rung from the end of Matins until after the *Angelus* of the morning. This may be observed according to the custom of the place.

The Religious, who, on account of their occupations, cannot go to the infirmary at the sound of the bell, shall pray during some space of time when they hear it rung, thus rendering their sick Sister this duty of charity. The Mistresses of the classes shall cause the same to be done by the boarders and penitents.

If the sick person enters her agony during the night, those of the Religious who will not be inconvenienced by it, shall be summoned, that they may come to pray for her, which should be done without ringing or disturbing those who are not strong.

Whilst the prayers are said during the agony, a blessed candle is given to the sick person, to oppose the spirit of darkness, to put him to flight, in virtue of the blessing it has received, and to acknowledge oneself a criminal before God, making a reparation of honour to His justice.

Prayers for the Agonizing.

Lord have mercy on her.
Christ have mercy on her.
Lord have mercy on her.
Holy Mary, pray for her.
All ye holy Angels and Archangels,
Holy Abel,
All ye choirs of the Just,
Holy Abraham,
St. John Baptist,
St. Joseph,
All ye holy Patriarchs and Prophets,
St. Peter,
St. Paul,
St. Andrew,
St. John,
All ye holy Apostles and Evangelists,
All ye holy disciples of our Lord,
All ye holy Innocents,
St. Stephen,
St. Lawrence,
All ye holy Martyrs,
St. Sylvester,
St. Gregory,
St. Augustine,
All ye holy Bishops and Confessors,
St. Benedict,
St. Francis,
All ye holy Monks and Hermits,
St. Mary Magdalen,
St. Lucy,
All ye holy Virgins and Widows,
All ye men and women, Saints of God,

Pray for her.

Intercede for her.
Be merciful,
Spare her, O Lord.
Be merciful,
Graciously hear her, O Lord.

Be merciful,
O Lord, deliver her,
From Thy wrath,
From the peril of death,
From an evil death,
From the pains of hell,
From all evil,
From the power of the devil,
Through Thy Nativity,
Through Thy Cross and Passion,
Through Thy Death and Burial,
Through Thy glorious Resurrection,
Through Thine admirable Ascension,
Through the grace of the Holy Ghost the Comforter,
In the day of judgment,
We sinners,
Beseech Thee, hear us.
That Thou spare her,
We beseech Thee, hear us.
Lord have mercy.
Christ have mercy.
Lord have mercy.

O Lord, deliver her.

Go forth, Christian soul, from this world, in the name of God the Father Almighty, who created thee; in the name of Jesus Christ, the Son of the living God, who suffered for thee; in the name of the Holy Ghost, who was poured out upon thee; in the name of the Angels and Archangels; in the name of the Thrones and Dominations; in the name of the Principalities and Powers; in the name of the Cherubim and Seraphim; in the name of the Patriarchs and Prophets; in the name of the holy Apostles and Evangelists; in the name of the holy Martyrs and Confessors; in the name of the holy Monks and Hermits; in the name of the holy Virgins and of all the Saints of God: may thy place be this day in peace, and thine abode in holy Sion. Through Christ our Lord. Amen.

O God most merciful, O God most clement, O God who according to the multitude of Thy mercies blottest out the sins of the penitent, and graciously remittest the guilt of their past offences, look favourably upon this Thy servant, N., and in Thy mercy hear her begging, with the whole confession of her heart, for the remission of all her sins. Renew in her, O most loving Father, whatsoever hath been corrupted through human frailty, or violated through the deceit of the devil; and associate her as a member of redemption, to the unity of the body of the Church. Have pity, Lord, on her sighs; have pity on her tears; and admit her, whose only hope is in Thy mercy, to the sacrament of Thy reconciliation. Through Christ our Lord. Amen.

I commend thee to Almighty God, dear sister, and commit thee to Him whose creature thou art; that, when thou shalt have paid the debt of humanity by death, thou mayest return to thy Maker, who formed thee of the dust of the earth. As thy soul goeth forth from the body, may the bright company of Angels meet thee; may the judicial senate of Apostles greet thee; may the triumphant army of white-robed Martyrs come out to welcome thee; may the band of glowing Confessors, crowned with lilies, encircle thee; may the choir of Virgins, singing jubilees, receive thee; and the embrace of a blessed repose fold thee in the bosom of the Patriarchs; with a mild and cheerful countenance may Jesus Christ appear to thee, and may He award thee a place among them that stand before Him for ever. Mayest thou be a stranger to all that is punished with darkness, chastised with flames, and condemned to torments. May foulest Satan, with his crew, give way before thee; may he tremble at thy coming among Angels that attend thee, and flee away into the vast chaos of eternal night. Let God arise, and let His enemies be scattered; let them also that hate Him flee before His face. As the smoke vanisheth, so let them fall away; and as wax melteth before the fire, so let the wicked perish at the presence of God; but let the just rejoice and exult before Him. May then all the legions of hell be confounded and put to shame, and the ministers of Satan never dare to stop thy way. May Christ, who was crucified for thee,

G

deliver thee from torments. May Christ, who vouchsafed to die for thee, deliver thee from everlasting death. May Christ, the Son of the living God, place thee within the ever-verdant gardens of His paradise, and may He, the True Shepherd, acknowledge thee among His sheep. May He absolve thee from all thy sins, and place thee at His right hand in the lot of His elect. Mayest thou behold thy Redeemer face to face; and, standing always in His presence, gaze with blessed eyes on the open vision of truth. And, placed thus among the troops of the blessed, mayest thou enjoy the sweetness of divine contemplation for ever and ever. Amen.

Receive, O Lord, Thy servant into the place of salvation, of which she hath no hope but in Thy mercy.
R. Amen.
Deliver, O Lord, the soul of Thy servant from all the dangers of hell, and from the snares of torment, and from all tribulations.
R. Amen.
Deliver, O Lord, the soul of Thy servant, as Thou deliveredst Enoch and Elias from the common death of the world.
R. Amen.
Deliver, O Lord, the soul of Thy servant, as Thou deliveredst Noah from the flood.
R. Amen.
Deliver, O Lord, the soul of Thy servant, as Thou deliveredst Abraham from Ur of the Chaldeans.
R. Amen.
Deliver, O Lord, the soul of Thy servant, as Thou deliveredst Job from all his sufferings.
R. Amen.
Deliver, O Lord, the soul of Thy servant, as Thou deliveredst Isaac from being sacrificed by the hand of his father Abraham.
R. Amen.
Deliver, O Lord, the soul of Thy servant, as Thou deliveredst Lot from Sodom and from the flame of fire.
R. Amen.

Deliver, O Lord, the soul of Thy servant, as Thou deliveredst Moses from the hands of Pharaoh, King of the Egyptians.

R. Amen.

Deliver, O Lord, the soul of Thy servant, as Thou deliveredst Daniel from the den of lions.

R. Amen.

Deliver, O Lord, the soul of Thy servant, as Thou deliveredst the three children from the burning fiery furnace, and from the hands of the wicked king.

R. Amen.

Deliver, O Lord, the soul of Thy servant, as Thou deliveredst Susanna from false accusation.

R. Amen.

Deliver, O Lord, the soul of Thy servant, as Thou deliveredst David from the hand of King Saul, and from the hand of Goliah.

R. Amen.

Deliver, O Lord, the soul of Thy servant, as Thou deliveredst Peter and Paul out of prison.

R. Amen.

And as Thou deliveredst Thy most blessed Virgin and Martyr, Thecla, from three most cruel torments, so vouchsafe to deliver the soul of this Thy servant, and make it rejoice with Thee in the delights of heaven.

R. Amen.

We commend to Thee, O Lord, the soul of Thy servant, N., and we beseech Thee, O Lord Jesus Christ, Saviour of the world, that Thou wouldst not refuse to receive into the bosom of Thy Patriarchs, a soul for whose sake Thou didst mercifully come down upon earth. Remember, O Lord, she is Thy creature, not made by strange gods, but by Thee, the only living and true God; for there is no other God beside Thee, and none that doeth according to Thy works. Rejoice her soul, O Lord, with Thy presence, and remember not the iniquities and excesses which, through the violence of anger or the heat of evil passion, she hath at any time committed. For although she hath sinned she hath not denied the Father, and the Son, and the Holy Ghost, but hath believed, and hath had a zeal for God, and hath faithfully adored the Creator of all things.

Remember not, O Lord, we beseech Thee, the sins of her youth and her ignorances; but, according to Thy great mercy, be mindful of her in the brightness of Thy glory. Let the heavens be opened to her, let the angels rejoice with her. Receive Thy servant, O Lord, into Thy kingdom. Let St. Michael, the Archangel of God, Prince of the armies of Heaven, receive her. Let the holy angels of God come forth to meet her, and conduct her to the city of the heavenly Jerusalem. Let Blessed Peter the Apostle, to whom God gave the keys of the kingdom of Heaven, receive her. Let St. Paul the Apostle, who was counted worthy to be a vessel of election, assist her. Let St. John, the chosen Apostle of God, to whom were revealed the secrets of Heaven, intercede for her. Let all the Holy Apostles, to whom the Lord gave the power of binding and loosing, pray for her. Let all the Saints and Elect of God, who in this world have suffered torments for the name of Christ, intercede for her, that loosed from the bonds of the flesh she may attain unto the glory of the heavenly kingdom; through the grace of our Lord Jesus Christ, who, with the Father and the Holy Ghost, liveth and reigneth for ever and ever. R. Amen.

Litany of the Most Holy Name of Jesus.

Lord, have mercy on us.
Christ, have mercy on us.
Lord, have mercy on us.
Jesus, hear us.
Jesus, graciously hear us.
God the Father of Heaven, have mercy on us.
God the Son, Redeemer of the World,
God the Holy Ghost,
Holy Trinity, one God,
Jesus, Son of the living God,
Jesus, splendour of the Father,
Jesus, brightness of eternal light,

Jesus, King of Glory,
Jesus, Sun of Justice,
Jesus, Son of the Virgin Mary,
Jesus, most amiable,
Jesus, most admirable,
Jesus, mighty God,
Jesus, Father of the world to come,
Jesus, Angel of great counsel,
Jesus, most powerful,
Jesus, most patient,
Jesus, most obedient,
Jesus, meek and humble of heart,
Jesus, lover of chastity,
Jesus, lover of us,
Jesus, God of peace,
Jesus, Author of life,
Jesus, example of virtues,
Jesus, zealous lover of souls,
Jesus, our God,
Jesus, our refuge,
Jesus, Father of the poor,
Jesus, treasure of the faithful,
Jesus, Good Shepherd,
Jesus, true light,
Jesus, eternal wisdom,
Jesus, infinite goodness,
Jesus, our way and our life,
Jesus, joy of Angels,
Jesus, King of Patriarchs,
Jesus, Master of Apostles,
Jesus, Teacher of Evangelists,
Jesus, strength of Martyrs,
Jesus, light of Confessors,
Jesus, purity of Virgins,
Jesus, crown of all Saints,

Have mercy on us.

Be merciful unto us,
Spare us, O Jesus,
Be merciful unto us,
Graciously hear us, O Jesus.

From all evil, Jesus, deliver us.
From all sin,
From Thy wrath,
From the snares of the devil,
From the spirit of uncleanness,
From everlasting death,
From the neglect of Thy inspirations.
Through the mystery of Thy holy Incarnation,
Through Thy Nativity,
Through Thine infancy,
Through Thy most divine life,
Through Thy labours,
Through Thine agony and passion.
Through Thy Cross and dereliction,
Through Thy faintness and weariness,
Through Thy death and burial,
Through Thy resurrection,
Through Thine ascension,
Through Thy joys,
Through Thy glory,

Jesus, deliver us.

Lamb of God, who takest away the sins of the world,
Spare us, O Jesus,
Lamb of God, who takest away the sins of the world,
Graciously hear us, O Jesus.
Lamb of God, who takest away the sins of the world,
Have mercy on us, O Jesus.
Jesus, hear us.
Jesus, graciously hear us.

Let us pray.

O Lord Jesus Christ, who has said: Ask, and ye shall receive; seek, and ye shall find; knock, and it shall be opened unto you; give, we beseech Thee, to us who ask, the grace of Thy most Divine love, that with all our heart, words, and works, we may love Thee, and never cease to praise Thee.

Make us, O Lord, to have a perpetual fear and love of Thy Holy Name, for Thou never failest to govern those whom Thou dost solidly establish in Thy love, who livest and reignest for ever and ever. Amen.

If the sick person continues longer in her agony, the Passion, according to St. John, may be read, or the Rosary said. After which:

V. We adore Thee, O Christ, and we bless Thee.
R. Because by Thy Holy Cross Thou hast redeemed the world.

O God, who to redeem the world didst condescend to be born, circumcised, rejected by the Jews, betrayed by a kiss from Judas, bound, led like a lamb to the slaughter, and dragged ignominiously before Annas and Caiphas, Pilate and Herod; to be falsely accused, beaten with rods, blindfolded, crowned with thorns, and despoiled of Thy garments; to be nailed to a cross in company with malefactors and to be pierced with a lance. O Lord, by all these sacred sorrows, which, unworthy as I am, I hold in veneration, and by Thy most holy Cross and death, deliver me from eternal woe.

R. Deliver Thy servant and vouchsafe to conduct her as Thou didst conduct the good thief who was crucified with Thee; who with the Father and Holy Ghost livest and reignest world without end. Amen.

If the agony continue the following psalm may be said:—

Psalm CXVII.

Confitemini Domino, quoniam bonus: quoniam in sæculum misericordia ejus.

Dicat nunc Israel, quoniam bonus: quoniam in sæculum misericordia ejus.

Dicat nunc domus Aaron: quoniam in sæculum misericordia ejus.

Dicant nunc qui timent

1. O praise ye the Lord, for he is good: for his mercy endureth for ever.

2. Let Israel now say, that he is good: that his mercy endureth for ever.

3. Let the house of Aaron now say: that his mercy endureth for ever.

4. Let them that fear the

Dominum: quoniam in sæculum misericordia ejus.	Lord now say: that his mercy endureth for ever.
De tribulatione invocavi Dominum: et exaudivit me in latitudine Dominus.	5. In my trouble I called upon the Lord: and the Lord heard and enlarged me.
Dominus mihi adjutor: non timebo quid faciat mihi homo.	6. The Lord is my helper: I will not fear what man can do unto me.
Dominus mihi adjutor: et ego despiciam inimicos meos.	7. The Lord is my helper: and I will look down upon mine enemies.
Bonum est confidere in Domino, quam confidere in homine.	8. It is better to trust in the Lord than to put confidence in man.
Bonum est sperare in Domino, quam sperare in principibus.	9. It is better to trust in the Lord than to put confidence in princes.
Omnes gentes circuierunt me; et in nomine Domini quia ultus sum in eos.	10. All nations compassed me about; and in the name of the Lord I have been revenged upon them.
Circumdantes circumdederunt me: et in nomine Domini quia ultus sum in eos.	11. Surrounding me, they compassed me about: and in the name of the Lord I have been revenged upon them.
Circumdederunt me sicut apes, et exarserunt sicut ignis in spinis: et in nomine Domini quia ultus sum in eos.	12. They gathered about me like bees, and burned like fire among thorns: and in the name of the Lord I have been revenged upon them.
Impulsus eversus sum ut caderem: et Dominus suscepit me.	13. I was sore pressed and overthrown that I might fall: but the Lord held me up.
Fortitudo mea, et laus mea Dominus: et factus est mihi in salutem.	14. The Lord is my strength and my praise: and he is become my salvation.
Vox exultationis et salutis, in tabernaculis justorum.	15. The voice of joy and salvation, is in the tabernacles of the just.
Dextera Domini fecit virtutem, dextera Domini exaltavit me: dextera Domini fecit virtutem.	16. The right hand of the Lord hath done mightily, the right hand of the Lord hath exalted me: the right hand

Non moriar, sed vivam: et narrabo opera Domini.

Castigans castigavit me Dominus: et morti non tradidit me.

Aperite mihi portas justitiæ; ingressus in eas confitebor Domino: hæc porta Domini, justi intrabunt in eam.

Confitebor tibi, quoniam exaudisti me: et factus es mihi in salutem.

Lapidem, quem reprobaverunt ædificantes, hic factus est in caput anguli.

A Domino factum est istud, et est mirabile in oculis nostris.

Hæc est dies, quam fecit Dominus: exultemus, et lætemur in ea.

O Domine, salvum me fac: O Domine, bene prosperare: benedictus qui venit in nomine Domini.

Benediximus vobis de domo Domini: Deus Dominus, et illuxit nobis.

Constituite diem solemnem in condensis, usque ad cornu altaris.

Deus meus es tu, et confitebor tibi: Deus meus es tu, et exaltabo te.

Confitebor tibi, quoniam

of the Lord hath done mightily.

17. I shall not die but live: and shall declare the works of the Lord.

18. The Lord hath chastened and corrected me: but he hath not given me over unto death.

19. Open to me the gates of justice; I will go into them, and give praise unto the Lord: this is the gate of the Lord, the just shall enter into it.

20. I will praise thee, for thou hast heard me: and art become my salvation.

21. The stone which the builders rejected, the same is become the head of the corner.

22. This is the Lord's doing, and it is marvellous in our eyes.

23. This is the day which the Lord hath made: let us be glad, and rejoice therein.

24. O Lord, save me: O Lord, give good success: blessed be he that cometh in the name of the Lord.

25. We have blessed you out of the house of the Lord: the Lord is God, and he hath shone upon us.

26. Appoint a solemn day, with shady boughs, even to the horn of the altar.

27. Thou art my God, and I will praise thee: thou art my God, and I will exalt thee.

28. I will praise thee, for

exaudisti me: et factus est mihi in salutem.

Confitemini Domino, quoniam bonus: quoniam in sæculum misericordia ejus.

Gloria Patri, &c.

thou hast heard me: and art become my salvation.

29. O praise ye the Lord, for he is good: for his mercy endureth for ever.

Glory be, &c.

Three Devout and Profitable Prayers for the Agony.

Lord have mercy, &c.
Christ have mercy, &c.
Lord have mercy, &c.
Our Father. Hail Mary.

Let us pray.

O Lord Jesus Christ, through Thy most sacred agony and prayer, wherein Thou madest supplication for us on Mount Olivet, when Thy sweat became as drops of blood trickling down upon the ground; vouchsafe, I beseech Thee, to offer and present to God the Father Almighty, for the abundance of all the sins of this Thy servant, N., the abundance of Thy bloody sweat which from anguish of fear Thou didst shed so abundantly for us; and deliver her at this hour of death from all the pain and anguish which for her sins she fears she hath deserved. Who with the Father and the Holy Ghost livest and reignest God for ever and ever. Amen.

Lord have mercy, &c.
Our Father. Hail Mary.

O Lord Jesus Christ, who didst vouchsafe to die upon the cross for us; vouchsafe, I beseech Thee, to offer and present to God the Father Almighty, for the soul of this Thy servant, N., all the bitterness of Thy pains and sufferings endured upon the cross for us miserable sinners, and chiefly at that hour when Thy most holy soul departed out of Thy sacred body; and deliver her at this hour of her death from all the pains and sufferings which for her sins she fears she hath deserved. Who with the Father and the Holy Ghost livest and reignest God for ever and ever. Amen.

Lord have mercy, &c.

Our Father. Hail Mary.

O Lord Jesus Christ, who by the mouth of the prophet hast said: I have loved thee with an everlasting love, therefore have I drawn thee to Myself, taking pity on thee; vouchsafe, I beseech thee, to offer and present to God the Father Almighty, for the soul of Thy servant, N., that same love which drew Thee down from heaven to earth to bear the bitterness of Thy sufferings; and deliver her from all the pains and sufferings which for her sins she fears she hath deserved. Oh, save her soul at this hour of its departure. Open to her the gate of life, and make her to rejoice with Thy saints in glory everlasting. O Lord Jesus Christ, most merciful, who didst redeem us by Thy most precious blood, have mercy on the soul of this Thy servant, and vouchsafe to admit it to the ever-verdant gardens of Paradise, that it may live to Thee in that inseparable love by which Thou art bound to Thine elect, and they to Thee eternally. Who with the Father and the Holy Ghost livest and reignest God for ever and ever. Amen.

Of the Death.

If there is nothing more desirable than a death precious before God, it is most important when the soul is ready to go to Him who is the centre of all her desires, that she should be more than ever fervent and watchful. Therefore, as the sick cannot in this extremity act with their usual freedom and strength of mind, the Priest, and the Religious, who assist, should charitably supply for this. Mass shall be said to obtain for her the grace of final perseverance, through the merits of Jesus Christ. Nevertheless, short and fervent acts should be suggested to her, such as:

I believe, Lord, help me.

Jesus, Son of David, have pity on me.

Nothing that I will, my God, but all that Thou willest.

O good Jesus, my refuge and my peace, defend me and forgive me.

My God, place Thy Cross and Thy Passion between Thy judgment and my soul.

Holy Mary, Mother of grace and mercy, defend me from my enemy.

St. Michael, combat for me.

My holy Angel Guardian, assist me.

Holy Martyrs, pray for me.

May all the holy Virgins and Widows come to receive my soul, when it leaves my body.

Into Thy hands, O Lord, I commend my spirit.

When the dying Sister has lost her speech, and that it is thought she can no longer hear, it is best to pray for her, endeavouring to obtain for her a good death, asking of God the pardon of her sins, strength in her sufferings, and mercy in the hour of her judgment. Nevertheless, the following acts should be whispered into her ear from time to time, because it often happens that the sick can hear and understand quite well, although unable to give any sign of this :

"I believe, my God, I hope, I love, I ask Thy pardon ; Thy will be done, I abandon myself to Thee, I desire Thee ;"—mingling with these prayers, the sacred names, Jesus, Mary ; Holy Virgin, pray for me ; My Jesus, receive my spirit.

When she is breathing her last, Jesus, Jesus, Jesus, should be repeated in a loud voice.

After the Death.

As soon as the sick person has expired, the Infirmarian, or another Sister, closes her eyes and mouth ; the Community is summoned, if the Sisters are not already in the infirmary, by tolling five strokes on the Church bell, unless it be in the night.

The Confessor, or, in his absence, the Superior, says aloud : *Subvenite Sancti Dei.* The Religious continue :

Occurrite, Angeli Domini, suscipientes animam ejus.*
Offerentes eam in conspectu Altissimi.

V. Suscipiat te Christus qui vocavit te, et in sinum Abrahæ Angeli deducant te.* Suscipientes animam ejus, offerentes in conspectu Altissimi. Requiem æternam, &c.,
* Offerentes, &c.

V. Kyrie eleison.
R. Christe eleison.
V. Kyrie eleison. Pater noster, &c., *in secret.*
V. Et ne nos inducas in tentationem.
R. Sed libera nos a malo.
V. Requiem æternam dona ei, Domine.
R. Et lux perpetua luceat ei.
V. A porta inferi.
R. Erue, Domine, animam ejus.
V. Requiescat in pace.
R. Amen.
V. Domine, exaudi orationem meam.
R. Et clamor meus ad te veniat.
V. Dominus vobiscum.
R. Et cum spiritu tuo.

Oremus.

Tibi, Domine, commendamus animam famulæ tuæ N. . . . matris (vel sororis) nostræ, ut defuncta sæculo tibi vivat, et quæ per fragilitatem humanæ conversationis peccata, commisit, tu venia misericordissimæ pietatis absterge. Per Christum Dominum nostrum.

Bells to be rung at the Death.

After this prayer, the Confessor, having sprinkled the body with holy water in the form of a cross, shall be conducted to the door of the enclosure by those who brought him in. The Infirmarian gives notice at once to the Sister Sacristan to ring the death bell, which is six strokes at three times, two at each, leaving the space of a *Requiem* between each two, after which thirty strokes are tolled, leaving also the space of a *Requiem* between each stroke; then a peal is rung for at least a quarter of an hour, if it be day, if not, as soon as it can be done. Those who have not been able to assist at the decease, shall place themselves on their knees at the sound of the bell, raise their hearts to God, and say a *De profundis*, or *Pater* and *Ave* for the repose of the soul of the deceased; and the Mistresses of the classes shall have these prayers said by the boarders and penitents.

Directions for Laying out the Body.

Some time after the death the Sister Infirmarian or another lays out the deceased Sister, taking care not to fasten down her arms; she clothes her in the ordinary habit, with the mantle, leaves the face, hands and feet uncovered (unless some reason prevents this), joins the hands, and places in them a little crucifix, and the vows of her profession. When the deceased is in the coffin, the Infirmarian surrounds it with a white sheet, which she covers with flowers, if possible, and places also a crown of flowers on her head.

A black veil is put on the Lay Sisters, and a white one on the Sisters Tourières, with the habit of the Order, if they have made their profession.

As soon as the Sister has breathed her last, the Infirmarian lights two wax candles, places holy water by the deceased, and a crucifix at her head; four Religious, who are changed from hour to hour, say psalms aloud, or recite prayers by her.

The Assistant makes a list of the Sisters who are to pray by the corpse, in order to give notice to each one of the hour at which she is to go.

The body ought to be exposed in a Mortuary Chapel, or in the ante-choir, or even in the choir, if such is the custom.

In this last case, a priest ought to preside at the ceremony of the removal of the body.

On Sundays and Holidays, the body ought not to be exposed in the choir.

If it happened, on account of some particular illness, that the deceased could not be exposed with her face uncovered, the coffin should be closed and covered with a pall.

The Religious of the choir are carried by Sisters of the same rank; the Lay Sisters (because the black veil is given them) are carried by two Sisters of the choir, assisted by Lay Sisters; the choir Sisters placing themselves at the head of the coffin. The novices and Sister Tourières are carried, if possible, by Lay Sisters.

The Removal of the Body.

At the hour named for the removal of the body (whether it be at the time of the burial or earlier), a peal is rung for the space of half a quarter of an hour, to assemble the Community in the choir. The Sister Sacristan distributes the candles, then, if there are no acolytes to accompany the priest, she takes the cross, and two novices the candlesticks; the Superior gives the sign, all go in procession to the place where the body is, where the Religious light their candles, and arrange themselves on each side; those who are to carry the corpse remain near, and if there is no acolyte, one of the last in rank takes the holy water. The priest, standing at the foot of the coffin, says the prayer as in the *Ritual*, and when he intones *Exultabunt*, the coffin is taken up, the procession advances, and the priest walks last of all, conducting the body, which ought to be immediately behind him. At the end of the *Exultabunt*, the chanters intone the *Miserere*, and afterwards the *Subvenite*.

The body is placed in the middle of the choir; the holy water ought to be near, and four white wax candles in black candlesticks, two on each side, with a crucifix at the head of the coffin.

The Sister Sacristan takes care to give the Celebrant the name of the deceased, that he may name her in the prayers of the Mass, the Office, and the Burial. The altar is dressed in black ; six candles are lighted upon it during the Mass, and whilst the Ecclesiastics are performing the ceremony.

It is a general rule, when the Office is said for one person in particular, the versicles and the responses should be in the singular, and in the plural when it is said for several, which is understood when there are several prayers said or only one for all. In *Requiem* Masses, the prayers are always said in the plural, except on the day of the death, or on an anniversary of one person in particular, when the singular is used.

The Bells which should be rung.

During the four-and-twenty hours or thereabouts that the body should be kept in the house, a peal is rung for about a quarter of an hour, a little after the *Angelus* of the morning, noon, and evening ; a peal is also rung during about half a quarter of an hour before the entrance of the Ecclesiastics, finishing when they enter the choir.

When the coffin is taken up to be carried out of the Church, the bell is again rung until the end of the burial.

The Ecclesiastical Superior sings the *Requiem* Mass, and performs the burial service (or the Confessor in his absence), the Ecclesiastics who assist him, say Mass in the morning for the deceased, and the *honorarium* is given to them, according to the custom of the place.

If the burial is in the afternoon, the *Requiem* Mass could be sung the following day, if the rank of the feast allows it.

Immediately after the death of a Religious, the Assistant, or another Sister who is appointed to do so, writes the death bills and gives them to the Sister Econome, who takes care to send them to the churches and communities in the town as soon as possible, to procure prayers for the deceased. They are written thus :

" Rev. —. You are very humbly requested, by the Religious of Our Lady of Charity of the Good Shepherd, to recommend to God in the Holy Sacrifice, Communions, and prayers, the soul of their dear Sister Mary . . . . . Religious of the Choir (or Lay Sister), departed the ...., fortified with the Holy Sacraments of the Church, aged ...., and in religion .... of their house of ...., this .... day of the month of .... of the year ,.......... *Requiescat in pace."*

The Superior gives notice of the death to the houses of the Institute, that the suffrages of the Order may be offered for the deceased.

The Burial.

At the hour of the burial, which should be, if possible, in the morning, in order that Mass may be said in the presence of the body, the Celebrant, having put aside his chasuble and maniple, puts on a black cope, and then, accompanied by the Deacon and Subdeacon in the usual vestments, excepting the maniple, he enters the choir, preceded by a clerk, who carries the crucifix, the thurifer who carries the thurible, and some other priests. The Religious stand in front of their stalls, turned towards the altar, having the veil lowered they each hold a lighted wax candle.

The Clergy then sing the prayers of the Liturgy.

Towards the end of the response *Libera me Domine*, the thurifer brings the thurible to the Deacon, and the Deacon presents the incense-boat to the Priest, that he may bless the incense, after he has put it in the thurible, saying: *Ab illo benedicaris in cujus honorem cremaberis*. The response being finished, the Celebrant says, *Kyrie*, &c., the Clergy *Christe*, &c., *Kyrie*, &c., *Pater noster* in secret, during which, having received the Asperges brush from the hand of the Deacon, he sprinkles holy water round the body, beginning on the right side; the Deacon raises the end of the cope on one side, and the Subdeacon on the other (if it be not at the end of Mass, an acolyte assists the Priest and accompanies him on the right); passing before the cross, he makes a profound inclination to it, and his ministers a genuflection, returning on the left side, sprinkling the holy water three times on each side. Having returned to his place, he receives the thurible from the hand of the Deacon, and incenses the body in the same manner, as was said for the holy water; after which he takes his place again, and says (the Deacon and Subdeacon holding the book for him):

V. Et ne nos inducas in tentationem.
R. Sed libera nos a malo.
V. A porta inferi.
R. Erue, Domine, animam ejus.
V. Requiescat in pace.
R. Amen.
V. Domine, exaudi orationem meam.
R. Et clamor meus ad te veniat.
V. Dominus vobiscum.
R. Et cum spiritu tuo.

Oremus.

Deus, cui proprium est misereri semper, et parcere, te supplices exoramus pro anima famulæ tuæ, N., quam hodie de hoc sæculo migrare jussisti, ut non tradas eam in manus inimici, neque obliviscaris in finem; sed jubeas eam a sanctis Angelis suscipi, et ad patriam paradisi perduci; ut quia in te speravit, et credidit, non pœnas inferni sustineat, sed gaudia æterna possideat.   Per Christum Dominum nostrum.   R. Amen.

This prayer being said, a chanter intones the following antiphon, which is said or sung slowly, until the cemetery is reached.

ANT. In paradisum deducant te Angeli, in tuo adventu suscipiant te Martyres, et perducant te in civitatem sanctam Jerusalem.   Chorus Angelorum te suscipiat, et cum Lazaro quondam paupere æternam habeas requiem.

If the burial takes place within the enclosure, the Religious, as soon as the prayer *Deus cui proprium est* commences, make the genuflection altogether in their places; those who carry the cross and candlesticks go out first to proceed to the burial place, the others follow two and two in their rank, beginning with the novices. Those who are to carry the body take away the candles which are round it. The Superior walks immediately before the Ecclesiastics, who are followed by the corpse.

If the antiphon is not sufficient it may be repeated, and the following psalms said or sung until the moment when the body is put in the grave:

Psalm XLI.

Quemadmodum desiderat cervus ad fontes aquarium: ita desiderat anima mea ad te, Deus.

Sitivit anima mea ad Deum fortem vivum: quando veniam, et apparebo ante faciem Dei.

Fuerunt mihi lacrymæ meæ panes die ac nocte: dum dicitur mihi quotidie: Ubi est Deus tuus?

Hæc recordatus sum, et effudi in me animam meam: quoniam transibo in locum tabernaculi admirabilis, usque ad domum Dei.

In voce exultationis, et confessionis: sonus epulantis.

Quare tristis es, anima mea: et quare conturbas me?

Spera in Deo quoniam adhuc confitebor illi: salutare vultus mei, et Deus meus.

Ad meipsum anima mea conturbata est: propterea memor ero tui de terra Jor-

1. As the hart panteth after the fountains of water: so my soul panteth after thee, O God.

2. My soul hath thirsted after the strong living God; when shall I come and appear before the face of God?

3. My tears have been my bread day and night, whilst it is said to me daily, where is thy God?

4. These things I remembered, and poured out my soul in me: for I shall go over into the place of the wonderful tabernacle, even to the house of God:

5. With the voice of joy and praise; the noise of one feasting.

6. Why art thou sad, O my soul? and why dost thou trouble me?

7. Hope in God; for I will still give praise to him, the salvation of my countenance, and my God.

8. My soul is troubled within myself: therefore will I remember thee from the

danis, et Hermoniim a monte modico.

Abyssus abyssum invocat: in voce cataractarum tuarum.

Omnia excelsa tua, et fluctus tui: super me transierunt.

In die mandavit Dominus misericordiam suam: et nocte canticum ejus.

Apud me oratio Deo vitæ meæ: dicam Deo: Susceptor meus es.

Quare oblitus es mei: et quare contristatus incedo dum affligit me inimicus.

Dum confringuntur ossa mea: exprobraverunt mihi qui tribulant me inimici mei.

Dum dicunt mihi per singulos dies: Ubi est Deus tuus? quare tristis es, anima mea et quare conturbas me?

Spera in Deo, quoniam adhuc confitebor illi: salutare vultus mei et Deus meus.

Requiem æternam, &c.

Land of Jordan and Hermoniim, from the little hill.

9. Deep calleth on deep, at the noise of thy floodgates.

10. All thy heights and thy billows have passed over me.

11. In the day time the Lord hath commanded his mercy; and a canticle to him in the night.

12. With me is prayer to the God of my life. I will say to God, thou art my support.

13. Why hast thou forgotten me? and why go I mourning, whilst my enemy afflicteth me?

14. Whilst my bones are broken, my enemies who trouble me have reproached me.

15. Whilst they say to me, day by day, where is thy God? Why art thou cast down, O my soul? and why dost thou disquiet me?

16. Hope thou in God, for I will still give praise to him: the salvation of my countenance and my God.

Grant them eternal rest, &c.

Psalm LXIV.

Te decet hymnus Deus in Sion: et tibi reddetur votum in Jerusalem.

Exaudi orationem meam: ad te omnis caro veniat.

1. A hymn, O God, becometh thee in Sion: and a vow shall be paid to thee in Jerusalem.

2. O hear my prayer; all flesh shall come to thee.

Verba iniquorum prevaluerunt super nos: et impietatibus nostris tu propitiaberis.

Beatus quem elegisti et assumpsisti: inhabitabit in atriis tuis.

Replebimur in bonis domus tuæ: sanctum est templum tuum, mirabile in æquitate.

Exaudi nos, Deus salutaris noster: spes omnium finium terræ et in mare longe.

Præparans montes in virtute tua, accinctus potentia: qui conturbas profundum maris sonum fluctuum ejus.

Turbabuntur gentes et timebunt qui habitant terminos a signis tuis: exitus matutini et vespere delectabis.

Visitasti terram et inebriasti eam: multiplicasti locupletare eam.

Flumen Dei repletum est aquis parasti cibum illorum: quoniam ita est præparatio ejus.

Rivos ejus inebria multiplica genimina ejus: in stillicidiis ejus lætabitur germinans.

Benedices coronæ anni benignitatis tuæ: et campi tui replebuntur ubertate.

3. The words of the wicked have prevailed over us: and thou wilt pardon our transgressions.

4. Blessed is he whom thou hast chosen and taken to thee: he shall dwell in thy courts.

5. We shall be filled with the good things of thy house: holy is thy temple, wonderful in justice.

6. Hear us, O God our Saviour, *who art* the hope of all the ends of the earth, and in the sea afar off.

7. Thou who preparest the mountains by thy strength, being girded with power: who troublest the depth of the sea, the noise of its waves.

8. The gentiles shall be troubled, and they that dwell in the uttermost borders shall be afraid at thy signs: thou shall make the outgoings of the morning and of the evening to be joyful.

9. Thou hast visited the earth, and hast plentifully watered it; thou hast many ways enriched it.

10. The river of God is filled with water: thou hast prepared their food, for so is its preparation.

11. Fill up plentifully the streams thereof; multiply its fruits; it shall spring up and rejoice in its showers.

12. Thou shalt bless the crown of the year of thy goodness: and thy fields shall be filled with plenty.

Pinguescent speciosa deserti: et exultatione colles accingentur.	13. The beautiful places of the wilderness shall grow fat: and the hills shall be girded about with joy.
Induti sunt arietes ovium, et valles abundabunt frumento: clamabunt, etenim hymnum dicent.	14. The rams of the flock are clothed, and the vales shall abound with corn: they shall shout, yea, they shall sing a hymn.
Requiem æternam, &c.	Grant them eternal rest, O Lord.

Psalm CXXIX.

De profundis clamavi ad te Domine: Domine, exaudi vocem meam.

Fiant aures tuæ intendentes: in vocem deprecationis meæ.

Si iniquitates observaveris Domine: Domine, quis sustinebit?

Quia apud te propitiatio est: et propter legem tuam sustinui te, Domine.

Sustinuit anima mea in verbo ejus: speravit anima mea in Domino.

A custodia matutina usque ad noctem: speret Israel in Domino.

Quia apud Dominum misericordia: et copiosa apud eum redemptio.

Et ipse redimet Israel: ex omnibus iniquitatibus ejus.

Requiem æternam dona eis, Domine: et lux perpetua luceat eis.

The cross-bearer having arrived at the cemetery, places herself at a little distance from where the head of the corpse is to be put, and those who carry the candlesticks on either side of her; the Religious place themselves farther off. Those who carry the body set it down at the side of the grave with the feet to the east. The clerk who carries the crucifix places himself at the head, the Priest and ministers at the feet, and the rest of the clergy divide on the two sides of the grave, if it can be done.

Then the Celebrant blesses the grave, if it be not already blessed, which is not necessary when the cemetery has been consecrated.

Oremus.

Deus cujus miseratione animæ fidelium requiescunt hunc tumulum benedicere dignare, eique angelum tuum sanctum deputa custodem ; et quarum corpora hic sepeliuntur, animas earum ab omnibus absolve vinculis delictorum ; ut in te semper cum sanctis tuis sine fine lætentur. Per Christum, &c.

At the end of the prayer, the Celebrant blesses the incense as before, saying, *Ab illo*, &c., and, having received the Asperges brush from the hand of the deacon, he throws holy water, in the form of a cross, on the body of the deceased and into the grave, without moving from his place, and likewise incenses both in the form of a cross. Immediately the Superior (assisted by the infirmarian or by her aide), covers the face of the deceased with a white handkerchief, lowers her veil, and places on her a wooden heart, from the middle of which rises a cross, instead of a silver heart, which she removes. The undertakers are ready to close the coffin immediately, and to lower it into the grave. The V. *Requiem* is begun, even if the psalms are not finished, at the end of which the celebrant intones the antiphon :

ANT. Ego sum resurrectio et vita : qui credit in me, etiam si mortuus fuerit, vivet : et omnes qui vivit et credit in me, non morietur in æternam.

And the chanter the canticle :

Benedictus Dominus Deus Israel : quia visitavit et fecit redemptionem plebis suæ.

Et erexit cornu salutis nobis : in domo David pueri sui.

Sicut locutus est per os sanctorum : qui a sæculo sunt prophetarum ejus.

Salutem ex inimicis nostris : et de manu omnium qui oderunt nos.

Ad faciendam misericordiam cum patribus nostris: et memorari testamenti sui sancti.

Jusjurandum quod juravit ad Abraham patrem nostrum: daturum se nobis.

Ut sine timore de manu inimicorum nostrorum liberati: serviamus illi.

In sanctitate et justitia coram ipso: omnibus diebus nostris.

Et tu puer propheta Altissimi vocaberis: præibis enim ante faciem Domini, parare vias ejus.

Ad dandam scientiam salutis plebi ejus: in remissionem peccatorum eorum.

Per viscera misericordiæ Dei nostri: in quibus visitavit nos oriens ex alto.

Illuminare his qui in tenebris et in umbra mortis sedent: ad dirigendos pedes nostros in viam pacis.

Requiem æternam, &c.

ANT. Ego sum, &c.

Some earth is thrown into the grave while the canticle is being sung and the antiphon repeated, at the end of which the Celebrant says:

V. *Kyrie eleison.* The clergy, *Christe eleison.* The celebrant, *Kyrie eleison. Pater noster*, during which he sprinkles the grave.

V. Et ne nos inducas in tentationem.
R. Sed libera nos a malo.
V. A porta inferi.
R. Erue, Domine, animam ejus.
V. Requiescat in pace.
R. Amen.
V. Domine, exaudi orationem meam.
R. Et clamor meus ad te veniat.
V. Dominus vobiscum.
R. Et cum spiritu tuo.

Oremus.

Fac quæsumus, Domine, hanc cum famula tua defuncta, N., misericordiam, ut factorum suorum in pœnis non recipiat

vicem, quæ tuam in votis tenuit voluntatem ; ut sicut eam vera fides junxit fidelium turmis, ita illic eam tua miseratio societ angelicis choris. Per Christum Dominum nostrum. Amen.
V. Requiem æternam dona ei Domine.
R. Et lux perpetua luceat ei.
V. Requiescat in pace.
R. Amen.

The Celebrant again sprinkles holy water on the grave, and having begun the antiphon *Si iniquitates* (which should not be sung), he returns with the Ecclesiastics, saying the Psalm *De profundis.*

After the departure of the Priests and cantors, the Community remains in the cemetery to throw holy water into the grave, and say the *De profundis*, at the end of which the Superior says the prayer :

Absolve, quæsumus, Domine, animam famulæ tuæ, N., sororis nostræ (vel matris), ut defuncta sæculo tibi vivat : et quæ per fragilitatem, carnis humana conversatione commisit, tu venia misericordissimæ pietatis absterge. Per Christum Dominum nostrum. Amen.

The Sisters extinguish their candles, except the two who accompany the cross, who do not either sprinkle the grave with holy water. The sign being given, they return to the choir in procession, and after a few prayers retire.

The Prayers and Suffrages for the Deceased Sisters.

On the day of the burial neither the *Magnificat* at Vespers nor the *Stabat* are sung ; nevertheless, if it were a Sunday or Holiday, and that the body were not in the choir, the Office of the day is sung as usual ; and if the Office for the deceased be transferred, the *Magnificat* is not sung at Vespers on that day either.—Care should be taken to give notice of the death to the relations of the deceased, as well as the time of the service and burial.

In the evening, after the burial, the Sisters say the whole Office of the Dead, unless the Superior thinks it better to leave Lauds till the next morning.

They have the service as soon as they can, observing to place no representation, or silver candlesticks, unless it were at a service for some secular person.

In the evening of the day of the burial a volley should be rung for the space of a quarter of an hour, after the *Angelus*.

On Sundays and ordinary feasts the obsequies may be performed, and the Solemn *Requiem* Mass said, having first said that of the Office of the day.

During the last days of Holy Week, the bell is not rung for the prayers and burial.

From the day of the decease, or the next day, an alms shall be given for a meal (for a poor girl) for thirty days, or else thirty pence shall be given to the poor, according to the order of the Superior.

They should have thirty Masses said for the deceased, and the Sisters for thirty days say a *De profundis*, with the prayer *Quæsumus, Domine*, after the Community Mass; if a solemn feast occur, or that there is Exposition of the Blessed Sacrament during the thirty days, it is said in secret. The Lay Sisters and Sister Tourières say every day a *Pater* and *Ave* for her.

If the Superior dies in office, the *De profundis* is said for her during a year.

The thirty Masses ought to be said at a privileged altar; if there is not one at the Convent, they should be said at a privileged altar in the town, if there is one, or else by a priest who has received this privilege from Rome.

A general Communion is offered by the Community for the deceased on the day of the burial. Thirty days after a Low Mass shall be said for her, and the Community shall communicate at it; besides this, three other general Communions shall be offered for her, of the ordinary ones of the Community, made during the thirty days. The Mistresses of the Classes shall also cause the *De profundis* to be said by the penitents during the same space of time.

The Office of the anniversary should be said exactly at the end of the year, if it can be. The Vigils, with three lessons are recited, and the prayer, *Deus indulgentiarum*, as it is said in the Breviary. The *Requiem* Mass is sung, and the general Communion offered.

After the death of the Sisters, at the foot of the page on which their Vows are written, the year, the day, and where they died, with the place where they are buried, should be entered, and an abridgment of the principal virtues which have shone in them.

When the news of a decease of a Sister of the Province is received, the Holy Sacrifice of the Mass is offered for her, at the end of which the *De profundis*, and prayer *Absolve*, are said; the Rosaries, prayers, and other good works which are done in the Community are applied to her, and the intention of a general Communion is given to her as soon as possible. The Office for the Dead of one Nocturn is said for her, the Lay Sisters and Sisters Tourières saying nine *Paters* and *Aves*. The houses of the Province in which a Sister dies are alone under *obligation* to give suffrages to the deceased. At the other Convents when the death is announced, a general Communion shall be offered for the deceased, with a *De profundis*, and once a month a Mass shall be said for all the Sisters who have died during the month.

The Mother House has a Mass said for each Religious who dies in the Institute.

At the decease of the near relations of the Religious, a Mass may be said for the repose of their soul, or at least a memento made in the Holy Sacrifice; the Superior has the *De profundis* and prayer *Absolve* said for them; and a general Communion is offered for them.

The Bells to be rung for the Office of the Dead which is said for the Religious, and on the Anniversary of the Founders.

For the Vespers of the day of the burial, the bell is rung from the beginning of the *Magnificat* of the Vespers of our Lady until the end, and for Matins from the *Benedictus* of Lauds until the Matins of the Dead.

When Lauds are said in the morning, the bell is rung during a short quarter of an hour, before assembling in the choir.

For Mass the bell is rung from the Psalm *Deus, Deus, meus*, until the end of the canticle *Ego dixi*, and tolled during ten or twelve verses of the Psalm *Laudate;* for the last bell thirty strokes are tolled during the *Benedictus*. When Lauds of the Dead are said the previous evening, the bell is rung for Mass from the first psalm of Sext, until the end of the last, and is tolled until the end of the prayer; for the last bell, thirty strokes are tolled at the Psalm *Beati omnes*, of None.

The bell is also rung during the *Libera*, which is sung at the end of the High Mass for the Dead.

On the anniversary the bell is rung at the *Magnificat*, and at Matins all through the *Benedictus;* for the High Mass, the first bell is rung from the beginning of the last psalm of Sext until the end of the antiphon, and is tolled until after the prayer; the last bell is tolled, as usual, at the third psalm of None.

For the Office of the Dead which is said at the beginning of the month, and for that which is said at the death of the Sisters, the bell is rung for Vespers and Matins as on the anniversary day.

When the Last Sacraments are administered to the Penitents.

When the penitents are ill, and they seem to be in danger of death, they shall be prepared to receive the Holy

Sacraments of Confession and Communion, at which last the Religious assist, if it can be. The Sister Sacristan shall provide all that is necessary for the occasion ; all the usual prayers shall be said, as well for the Holy Communion and Extreme Unction as for the Agony, each one striving to obtain for them, by prayers and good works, the disposition necessary to make this last passage happily. Those who have the charge of them shall pay particular attention that they have all the spiritual help they need, and that their corporal necessities are also very charitably provided for. The Sister Sacristan takes care to put a notice in the sacristy, in this form : " A poor penitent, who is at the point of death, is recommended to your prayers and holy sacrifices."

The Decease of the Penitents.

At the death of the penitents, children, or other persons who die in the Convent, the custom of the diocese in which it is established should be followed, for the bells and other arrangements.

The Sister Sacristan gives the name of the deceased to the Confessor, that he may name her at the burial, and at the Mass which should be said for her on the following morning, or the next free day. This Mass is not sung unless the Superior orders otherwise ; the Community shall communicate at it for the repose of her soul.

Benediction of the Blessed Sacrament.

January.

1. The Circumcision. Benediction in the afternoon.
6. The Epiphany. Exposition of the Blessed Sacrament in the morning.
29. Saint Francis of Sales. Benediction.

February.

2. The Purification. Benediction.
8. The Most Pure Heart of Mary. Titular feast; the most Blessed Sacrament is exposed from the first Vespers; and on the day of the feast from the morning meditation; during the octave the Blessed Sacrament is exposed at half-past two.

March.

13. Saint Euphrasia. Feast of our Venerable Mother Foundress. Very solemn Benediction.
19. Saint Joseph. Benediction.
25. The Annunciation. Exposition in the morning.

April or May.

Good Shepherd Sunday. Exposition of the Blessed Sacrament.

The custom of the diocese may be followed for the devotions for the month of May.

June.

24. Saint John Baptist. Solemn Benediction.
29. Saint Peter and Saint Paul. Very solemn Benediction.

July.

2. The Visitation of our Lady. Benediction.
22. Saint Mary Magdalen. Benediction.
31. Saint Ignatius. Very solemn Benediction.

August.

2. Feast of the Portiuncula. Benediction.
15. The Assumption of our Lady. Exposition of the Blessed Sacrament. Very solemn Benediction.
19. Our Venerable Father Eudes. Benediction.
28. Saint Augustine. Exposition of the Blessed Sacrament in the morning.

September.

8. The Nativity of the Blessed Virgin. Benediction.
29. Saint Michael. Benediction.

October.

15. Saint Teresa. Benediction.

November.

1. The Feast of All Saints. Exposition in the morning. Very solemn Benediction in the afternoon.
21. Feast of the Presentation of the Blessed Virgin. Exposition in the morning. Benediction in the afternoon.
25. Saint Catherine. Benediction.

December.

8. The Feast of the Immaculate Conception of the Blessed Virgin. Exposition in the morning.
25. The Nativity of our Lord. Very solemn Benediction in the afternoon and the following days.

Supplement.

The first Friday of every month. Benediction in honour of the Sacred Heart of Jesus.

During the whole of the devotion of the Forty Hours, Exposition of the most Blessed Sacrament.

Easter Sunday, and the two following days. Benediction.

The Ascension of our Lord. Exposition and very solemn Benediction.

Corpus Christi. Exposition and Benediction the whole octave.

Feast of the Sacred Heart of Jesus. Benediction on the eve and Exposition on the morning of the Feast.

During the octave. Exposition at half-past two.

Whit-Sunday and the two following days. Benediction.

Every Sunday in the year. Benediction.

The last day of the year. Benediction, during which the *Miserere* and *Te Deum* are sung.

Observations.

1. The custom of the place is to be observed for the singing at Benediction, the number of candles to be lighted at Exposition of the Blessed Sacrament, and at the Masses, the Church bells, &c.

2. The Roman Rite shall be followed, as far as possible, in all the ceremonies of the Church. In the dioceses where the devotion of the *Quarant' Ore* is ordered by the Bishop, and where the Roman Rite is observed, the processions will take place; the second day, the Mass *Pro pace* will be sung, but no Mass will be said at the altar where the Blessed Sacrament is exposed. The Office ought to be sung on these three days.

3. The first verse of the *Veni Creator* is sung kneeling at Vespers of the Feast of Pentecost and at Terce.

4. When the Blessed Sacrament is taken to the sick, the Sisters who accompany It wear mantles.

5. The veil is lowered a little for sermons.

6. The Sister who officiates goes to the lectern to sing the prayer after the *Inviolata*.

7. At Prime and Compline of the Divine Office the sign of the Cross is made, saying, *Adjutorium nostrum in nomine Domini*, and the same is done at the Ceremonies of Clothing and Profession.

8. A Decree of the Sacred Congregation of Rites, 3 June, 1892, ordained that at Benediction of the Blessed Sacrament during Paschal time, *Alleluia* should not be added, either to the versicles which follow the prayers in honour of the Blessed Virgin, such as the Litany, or the *Sub tuum*, or to the versicles which follow the *Te Deum*. Nevertheless, the *Alleluia* should be added to *Panem de cœlo*.

Extract from the Bull of Paul V.

INDULGENCES GRANTED TO RELIGIOUS OF BOTH SEXES, BY THE BRIEF OF PAUL V. OF MAY 23, 1606.

Plenary Indulgences.

1. *The day of their clothing* (Confession and Communion).
2. *The Profession day* (same conditions).
3. *On the principal feast of the Order* (they must go to Confession, Communion, and pray for the usual intentions).
4. *At the point of death*, if fortified by the Sacraments of Penance, the Eucharist, or, when that is impossible, if truly contrite, they invoke the Name of Jesus with their lips, or at least with their heart.
5. To all Religious of both sexes, who, with the leave of their respective Superiors, apply themselves during ten days to *the spiritual exercises*, making each day at least two hours of meditation on the last things, on the Passion of Our Lord, on the benefits received from God, &c., devoting themselves to other pious exercises, reciting vocal prayers, or else ejaculatory prayers, &c. They must also, during this retreat, make a general, annual, or at least their ordinary Confession, and shall go to Communion. *This Plenary Indulgence* may be gained each time they make their retreat *in the manner indicated above.*
6. Religious who, with the permission of the Sovereign Pontiff, or of their respective Superiors, go into the

countries of infidels or heretics, to preach the faith, can gain a Plenary Indulgence on the day of their departure, as also on the day of their arrival at their destination, provided they confess and communicate.

7. When the Superior, to obtain the happy success of the general visitation of his Order, prescribes forty hours' consecutive prayer, Religious of both sexes can gain a Plenary Indulgence; to obtain it, they must confess and communicate, and afterwards take part in the prescribed devotion, by spending two hours at intervals, praying for peace amongst Christian princes, &c., as also for increase of observance, and of regular discipline.

INDULGENCES OF THE STATIONS IN ROME.

All Religious of both sexes can gain these Indulgences, provided that, on the days mentioned in the Roman Missal, they visit devoutly their own church, and pray there for the intentions of the Sovereign Pontiff.

PARTIAL INDULGENCES.

1. *Sixty years and sixty quarantines*, to Religious of both sexes, if, having made during a month half an hour of mental prayer daily, they confess and communicate.

2. *Five years and five quarantines*, daily, if they recite five *Paters* and five *Aves* before the altar of their church. Religious of either sex who, for a legitimate reason and with authorization of Superiors, are travelling, can gain this Indulgence by saying the five *Paters* and the five *Aves* before any altar whatsoever.

3. *Three years and three quarantines*, each time that Religious men or women, with contrite heart, say their faults at the Chapter, accusing themselves of their faults and imperfections, hold spiritual conference together, and perform other acts of virtue.

Note.

1. Religious who, from illness or infirmity, are unable to visit a church, or fulfil the other conditions required, can, nevertheless, gain the Indulgences if they perform the practices of piety enjoined them by their confessor. (Indult of Pope Leo XIII., January 16, 1886).

2. The Indulgences and Privileges granted to a religious Order do not cease to exist, needless to say, if it is suppressed or illegally oppressed.

3. Religious of both sexes can gain the Indulgences common to all the faithful.

4. According to a Decree of the Sacred Congregation of Indulgences, dated July 16, 1887, members of any religious Order or Congregation whatever—whether their rule is approved by the Holy See, or only by the Bishops, whether they are bound by perpetual or temporary vows—can on no account whatever be received into the Third Order of Saint Francis of Assisium, that Association being destined only for the faithful living in the world. The same must be said, and for a similar reason, of all Third Orders.

Privileges

GRANTED TO CONVENTS OF THE REFUGE BY THE HOLY SEE, AND TO WHICH THE CONGREGATION OF OUR LADY OF CHARITY OF THE GOOD SHEPHERD OF ANGERS HAS A RIGHT, IN VIRTUE OF ART. 8 OF THE BRIEF FOR THE ERECTION OF THE GENERALATE, AND IN VIRTUE OF THE APPROBATION OF THE CONSTITUTIONS, MAY 22, 1897. (SEE CONSTIT. XXXII., ART. 6.)

I. *Plenary Indulgence* granted (on the usual conditions) to the faithful of both sexes, who shall visit one of our convent chapels. (Gregory XVI., June 18, 1844).

II. *Plenary Indulgence* granted to the Religious and inmates of our houses, on the following days:
The Second Sunday after Easter.
The First Sunday after the feast of Saint Chantal.
Saint Francis de Sales, January 29.
Saint Joseph, March 19.
Saint Mary Magdalen, July 22.
Saint Anne, July 26.
Death of the Venerable John Eudes, August 19.
Saint Catherine, November 25.
On the feasts of the Sacred Hearts of Jesus and of Mary, and on one of the seven days of their octaves. (Gregory XVI., June 18, 1844).

III. *The Indulgences of the Scapular of Mount Carmel*, attached to our silver hearts, on condition, nevertheless, that the remainder of what is prescribed for participating fully in the Indulgences of the Confraternity of Our Lady of Mount Carmel is fulfilled. (Pius IX., May 4, 1847.)

IV. *Plenary Indulgence* to all the Religious of our Order (on the usual conditions):

On the anniversary of their Clothing.

On the anniversary of their Profession.

Every month at the renewal of our holy vows.

Feast of the Holy Guardian Angels, October 2.

At the Communions of Rule which we make each month:

1. For the Holy Father, the Bishop and clergy of the Diocese.
2. For the union of our holy Order.
3. For the conversion of infidels and sinners.
4. For peace and union between Christian princes.
5. For the conversion of our penitents.
6. For our benefactors. (Pius IX., November 3, 1861.)

V. A *Plenary Indulgence* to all the Religious who, in public or private, at the end of their annual retreat, shall make the Seven Stations of Good Friday, in honour of the Passion of our Lord Jesus Christ, with prayers and meditations. (Pius IX., September 5, 1861.)

All these Indulgences are granted in perpetuity, and are applicable to the souls in purgatory.

VI. Privilege to add in the prayer *Confiteor Deo omnipotenti*, after the names of the Blessed Apostles, Saint Peter and Saint Paul, that of Saint Augustine, by these words: *Beati Patri nostro Augustino*, and *Beatum Patrum nostrum Augustinum.* (Pius IX., June 13, 1861.)

VII. Privilege to celebrate as double of the second class the feasts of the Presentation of our Lady, November 21, and of Saint Francis de Sales. (Pius IX., June 23, 1864.)

OBSERVATION.

Some objections having been made to us, regarding the various points prescribed in the *Directory*, relating to the recital and singing of the Office of the Blessed Virgin, chiefly on the addition of the *Alleluia* to the anthems, versicles, and responses of Paschal time, and other usages of the Institute, we have solicited the Sacred Congregation of Rites to grant the privileges mentioned in the following petition :

PETITION.

Convent General of the Good Shepherd.

Angers, July 26, 1899.

The Superior General of the Congregation of Our Lady of Charity of the Good Shepherd of Angers, very humbly petitions the Sacred Congregation of Rites to graciously accord to her Institute, the privilege of conforming on all points to the rules given for the recital of the Office of the Blessed Virgin, according to the different times of the year, in the *Directory of the Choir*, approved by his Eminence the Cardinal Protector of the Congregation, and in use in the Order from its foundation.

She petitions also for the privilege of taking solemn tones for the psalms of the Office on certain feasts, and to have some special music for the chant of the *Ave Maris Stella* at Vespers, and for the *Memento rerum conditor* at Terce.

MARY OF SAINT MARINE VERGER,
Superior General.

Annuimus juxta preces.
Romæ die 2 Aug., 1899.

L. ✠ S.   C. CARD. MAZZELLA, S.R.C.,
Præf. Protector.

Little Office of the Immaculate Conception.

At Matins.

Eja, mea labia, nunc annuntiate.	Come, my lips, and wide proclaim
Laudes et præconia Virginis beatæ.	The blessed Virgin's spotless fame.
V. Domina, in adjutorium meum intende.	V. O Lady, make speed to befriend me.
R. Me de manu hostium potenter defende.	R. From the hands of the enemy mightily defend me.
V. Gloria Patri, &c. Alleluia.	V. Glory be to the Father, &c. Alleluia.

From Septuagesima to Easter, instead of Alleluia *is said*:

Laus tibi, Domine, Rex æternæ gloriæ.	Praise be to thee, O Lord, King of everlasting glory.

HYMN.

Salve, mundi Domina,
Cœlorum Regina:
Salve, Virgo virginum,
Stella matutina.

Hail, Queen of the heavens,
Hail, mistress of earth!
Hail, Virgin most pure,
Of immaculate birth!

Salve, plena gratia,
Clara luce divina:
Mundi in auxilium,
Domina, festina.

Clear star of the morning,
In beauty enshrin'd!
O Lady, make speed
To the help of mankind.

Ab æterno Dominus
Te præordinavit
Matrem unigeniti
Verbi, quo creavit.

Thee God in the depth
Of eternity chose;
And form'd thee all fair
As his glorious Spouse;

Terram, pontum, æthera:
Te pulchram ornavit
Sibi Sponsam, quæ in
Adam non peccavit.
Amen.

V. Elegit eam Deus, et præelegit eam.
R. In tabernaculo suo habitare fecit eam.
V. Domina, exaudi orationem meam.
R. Et clamor meus ad te veniat.

Oremus.

Sancta Maria, Regina cœlorum, Mater Domini nostri Jesu Christi, et mundi Domina, quæ nullum derelinquis, et nullum despicis; respice me Domina, clementer oculo pietatis, et impetra mihi apud tuum dilectum Filium cunctorum veniam peccatorum: ut qui nunc tuam sanctam et immaculatam Conceptionem devoto affectu recolo, æternæ in futurum beatitudinis bravium capiam, ipso quem virgo peperisti donante Domino nostro Jesu Christo: qui cum Patre et Sancto Spiritu vivit et regnat, in Trinitate perfecta Deus in sæcula sæculorum. Amen.

V. Domina, exaudi orationem meam.
R. Et clamor meus ad te veniat.
V. Benedicamus Domino.
R. Deo gratias.

And call'd thee his Word's
Own Mother to be,
By whom he created
The earth, sky, and sea.
Amen.

V. God elected her, and pre-elected her.
R. He made her to dwell in his tabernacle.
V. O Lady, hear my prayer.
R. And let my cry come unto thee.

Let us pray.

Holy Mary, Queen of heaven, Mother of our Lord Jesus Christ, and Mistress of the world, who forsakest no one, and despisest no one; look upon me, O Lady, with an eye of pity, and entreat for me, of thy beloved Son, the forgiveness of all my sins; that, as I now celebrate with devout affection thy holy and Immaculate Conception, so, hereafter, I may receive the prize of eternal blessedness, by the grace of him whom thou, in virginity, didst bring forth, Jesus Christ our Lord; who, with the Father and the Holy Ghost, liveth and reigneth, in perfect Trinity, God, world without end. Amen.

V. O Lady, hear my prayer.
R. And let my cry come unto thee.
V. Let us bless the Lord.
R. Thanks be to God.

V. Fidelium animæ per misericordiam Dei requiescant in pace.
R. Amen.

V. May the souls of the faithful, through the mercy of God, rest in peace.
R. Amen.

At Prime.

V. Domina, in adjutorium meum intende.
R. Me de manu hostium potenter defende.
V. Gloria Patri. Alleluia.

V. O Lady, make speed to befriend me.
R. From the hands of the enemy mightily defend me.
V. Glory be to the Father, &c. Alleluia.

HYMN.

Salve, Virgo sapiens,
Domus Deo dicata,
Columna septemplici
Mensaque exornata.

Hail, Virgin most wise!
Hail, Deity's shrine!
With seven fair pillars,
And table divine!

Ab omni contagio
Mundi præservata:
Ante sancta in utero
Parentis, quam nata.

Preserv'd from the guilt
   Which hath come on us all
Exempt, in the womb,
   From the taint of the Fall!

Tu, Mater viventium,
Et porta es Sanctorum:
Nova stella Jacob,
Domina Angelorum.

O new star of Jacob!
   Of Angels the Queen!
O gate of the Saints!
   O mother of men!

Zabulo terribilis
Acies castrorum:
Portus et refugium
Sis Christianorum.
          Amen.

O terrible as
   The embattled array!
Be thou of the faithful
   The refuge and stay.
          Amen.

V. Ipse creavit illam in Spiritu Sancto.

V. The Lord Himself created her in the Holy Ghost.

R. Et effudit illam inter omnia opera sua.
V. Domina, exaudi, &c.
(cum Oratione ut supra).

R. And poured her out among all his works.
V. O Lady, hear, &c.
(with the Prayer and Versicles, as above).

At Terce.

V. Domina, in adjutorium meum intende.
R. Me de manu hostium potenter defende.
V. Gloria Patri. Alleluia.

V. O Lady, make speed to befriend me.
R. From the hands of the enemy mightily defend me.
V. Glory be to the Father, &c. Alleluia.

HYMN.

Salve, arca fœderis,
Thronus Salomonis,
Arcus pulcher ætheris,
Rubus visionis :

Hail, Solomon's throne!
Pure ark of the law!
Fair rainbow! and bush,
Which the Patriarch saw.

Virga frondens germinis :
Vellus Gedeonis :
Porta clausa numinis,
Favusque Samsonis.

Hail, Gedeon's fleece!
Hail, blossoming rod!
Samson's sweet honeycomb!
Portal of God!

Decebat tam nobilem
Natum, præcavere
Ab originali
Labe Matris Evæ ;

Well fitting it was,
That a Son so divine
Should preserve from all touch
Of original sin ;

Almam, quam elegerat,
Genitricem vere,
Nulli prorsus sinens
Culpæ subjacere.
Amen.

Nor suffer by smallest
Defect to be stain'd,
That Mother, whom he
For himself had ordain'd.
Amen.

V. Ego in altissimis habito.
R. Et thronus meus in columna nubis.
V. Domina, exaudi, &c. (*cum Oratione ut supra*).

V. I dwell in the highest.
R. And my throne is on the pillar of the clouds.
V. O Lady, hear, &c. (*with the Prayer and Versicles, as above*).

At Sext.

V. Domina, in adjutorium meum intende.
R. Me de manu hostium potenter defende.
V. Gloria Patri. Alleluia.

V. O Lady, make speed to befriend me.
R. From the hands of the enemy mightily defend me.
V. Glory be to the Father, &c. Alleluia.

HYMN.

Salve, Virgo puerpera, Templum Trinitatis, Angelorum gaudium, Cella puritatis:	Hail, virginal Mother! Hail, purity's cell! Fair shrine where the Trinity Loveth to dwell!
Solamen mœrentium, Hortus voluptatis: Palma patientiæ, Cedrus castitatis.	Hail, garden of pleasure! Celestial balm! Cedar of chastity! Martyrdom's palm.
Terra es benedicta Et sacerdotalis, Sancta et immunis Culpæ originalis.	Thou land set apart From uses profane! And free from the curse Which in Adam began!
Civitas altissimi, Porta orientalis: In te est omnis gratia, Virgo singularis. Amen.	Thou city of God! Thou gate of the east! In thee is all grace, O joy of the blest! Amen.

V. Sicut lilium inter spinas.
R. Sic amica mea inter filias Adæ.

V. Domina, exaudi, &c. (*cum Oratione ut supra*).

V. As the lily among the thorns.
R. So is my beloved among the daughters of Adam.

V. O Lady, hear, &c. (*with the Prayer and Versicles, as above*).

At None.

V. Domina, in adjutorium meum intende.
R. Me de manu hostium potenter defende.
V. Gloria Patri. Alleluia.

V. O Lady, make speed to befriend me.
R. From the hands of the enemy mightily defend me.
V. Glory be to the Father, &c. Alleluia.

HYMN.

Salve, urbs refugii, Turrisque munita David, propugnaculis Armisque insignita.	Hail, city of refuge! Hail, David's high tower! With battlements crown'd And girded with power!

In Conceptione
Charitate ignita,
Draconis potestas
Est a te contrita.

Fill'd at thy Conception
With love and with light,
The dragon by thee
Was shorn of his might.

O mulier fortis,
Et invicta Judith!
Pulchra Abisag virgo,
Verum fovens David!

O woman most valiant!
O Judith thrice blest!
As David was nursed
In fair Abishag's breast;

Rachel curatorem
Ægypti gestavit:
Salvatorem mundi
Maria portavit.

As the Saviour of Egypt
Upon Rachel's knee;
So the world's great Redeemer
Was cherished by thee.

Amen.

Amen.

V. Tota pulchra es, amica mea.
R. Et macula originalis numquam fuit in te.
V. Domina, exaudi, &c.
(*cum Oratione ut supra*).

V. Thou art all fair, my beloved.
R. And the original stain was never in thee.
V. O Lady, hear, &c.
(*with the Prayer and Versicles, as above*).

At Vespers.

V. Domina, in adjutorium meum intende.
R. Me de manu hostium potenter defende.
V. Gloria Patri. Alleluia.

V. O Lady, make speed to befriend me.
R. From the hands of the enemy mightily defend me.
V. Glory be to the Father, &c. Alleluia.

HYMN.

Salve, horologium
Quo retrogradiatur
Sol in decem lineis;
Verbum incarnatur.

Hail, dial of Achaz!
On thee the true sun
Told backward the course
Which from old he had run!

Homo ut ab inferis,
Ad summa attollatur,
Immensus ab Angelis
Paulo minoratur.

And, that man might be rais'd,
Submitting to shame,
A little more low
Than the Angels became.

Solis hujus radiis
Maria coruscat;
Consurgens aurora
In conceptu micat.

Lilium inter spinas,
Quæ serpentis conterat
Caput: pulchra ut luna
Errantes collustrat.
          Amen.

V. Ego feci in cœlis, ut oriretur lumen indeficiens.
R. Et quasi nebula texi omnem terram.
V. Domina, exaudi, &c.
(*cum Oratione ut supra*).

Thou, wrapt in the blaze
Of his infinite light,
Dost shine as the morn
On the confines of night;

As the moon on the lost
Through obscurity dawns;
The serpent's destroyer,
A lily 'mid thorns!
          Amen.

V. I made an unfailing light to arise in heaven.
R. And, as a mist, I overspread the whole earth.
V. O Lady, hear, &c.
(*with the Prayer and Versicles, as above*).

At Compline.

V. Convertat nos, Domina, tuis precibus placatus Jesus Christus Filius tuus.

R. Et avertat iram suam a nobis.
V. Domina, in adjutorium meum intende.
R. Me de manu hostium potenter defende.
V. Gloria Patri. Alleluia.

V. May Jesus Christ thy Son, reconciled by thy prayers, O Lady, convert our hearts.

R. And turn away his anger from us.
V. O Lady, make speed to befriend me.
R. From the hands of the enemy mightily defend me.
V. Glory be to the Father, &c. Alleluia.

HYMN.

Salve, Virgo florens,
Mater illibata,
Regina clementiæ,
Stellis coronata.

Super omnes Angelos
Pura, immaculata,
Atque ad regis dexteram
Stans veste deaurata.

Hail, Mother most pure!
Hail, Virgin renown'd!
Hail, Queen with the stars
As a diadem crown'd!

Above all the Angels
In glory untold,
Standing next to the King
In a vesture of gold!

Per te, Mater gratiæ,
Dulcis spes reorum,
Fulgens stella maris,
Portus naufragorum,

Patens cœli janua,
Salus infirmorum,
Videamus Regem
In aula Sanctorum.
    Amen.

O Mother of mercy!
O star of the wave!
O hope of the guilty!
O light of the grave!

Through thee may we come,
To the haven of rest;
And see heaven's King
In the courts of the blest!
    Amen.

V. Oleum effusum, Maria, nomen tuum.
R. Servi tui dilexerunt te nimis.
V. Domina, exaudi, &c. (*cum Oratione ut supra*).

V. Thy name, O Mary, is as oil poured out.
R. Thy servants have loved thee exceedingly.
V. O Lady, hear, &c. (*with the Prayer and Versicles, as above*).

The Commendation.

Supplices offerimus
Tibi, Virgo pia,
Hæc laudum præconia;
Fac nos ut in via

Ducas cursu prospero;
Et in agonia
Tu nobis assiste,
O dulcis Maria.

These praises and prayers
 I lay at thy feet,
O Virgin of virgins!
 O Mary most sweet!

Be thou my true guide
 Through this pilgrimage here;
And stand by my side
 When death draweth near.

R. Deo gratias.

R. Thanks be to God.

ANT. Hæc est virga in qua nec nodus originalis, nec cortex actualis culpæ fuit.

V. In conceptione tua Virgo Immaculata fuisti.

R. Ora pro nobis Patrem cujus Filium peperisti.

ANT. This is the rod in which was neither knot of original sin, nor rind of actual guilt.

V. In thy Conception, O Virgin! thou wast immaculate.

R. Pray for us to the Father, whose Son thou didst bring forth.

Oremus.

Deus, qui per immaculatam virginis Conceptionem dignum Filio tuo habitaculum præparasti: quæsumus ut qui ex morte ejusdem Filii tui prævisa, eam ab omni labe præservasti nos quoque mundos ejus intercessione ad te pervenire concedas. Per Dominum, &c. Amen.

Let us pray.

O God, who, by the Immaculate Conception of the Virgin, didst prepare a worthy habitation for thy Son, we beseech Thee that Thou, who, by the death of that same Son of Thine, foreseen by Thee, didst preserve her from every stain of sin, wouldst grant that by her intercession we also may be purified, and so come to Thee. Through the same Christ our Lord. Amen.

CONVENTS OF THE CONGREGATION

OF

Our Lady of Charity of the Good Shepherd of Angers.

FRANCE.

No.		Date of the foundation.	No.		Date of the foundation.
1.	Angers	1829, 31 July.	20.	Dôle	1844, 18 Dec.
	(Mother House).		21.	Loos	1845, 4 April.
2.	Poitiers	1833, 3 Dec.	22.	Saint-Omer —	22 Sept.
3.	Grenoble	— 20 Dec.	23.	Moulins	1846, 1 Sept.
4.	S.-Hilaire-S.-Florent		24.	Angoulême —	28 Oct.
		1835, 31 July.	25.	Annonay	1850, 20 Aug.
5.	Nancy	— 30 Nov.	26.	Arras	1852, 2 July.
6.	Amiens	1836, 9 Mar.	27.	Nazareth (near Angers)	
7.	Lille	— 15 Sept.			1852, 20 Dec.
8.	Le Puy-en-Velay		28.	Cholet	1859, 23 June.
		1837, 1 Jan.	29.	Orleans	1860, 1 May.
9.	Sens	— 15 May.	30.	Bastia (Corsica)	
10.	Reims	— 11 June.			1860, 15 Aug.
11.	Arles	— 25 Sept.	31.	Ecully	1867, 1 Mar.
12.	Chambéry (Savoy)		32.	Pau	1876, 11 Aug.
		1839, 12 Jan.	33.	Troyes	1879, 2 July.
13.	Perpignan	— 25 Jan.	34.	Cambrai	1880, 15 Oct
14.	Bourges	— 24 Oct.	35.	Le Hâvre	1895, 28 Oct.
15.	Nice	— 1 April.	36.	Lourdes	1898, 8 Dec.
16.	Avignon	— 9 May.	37.	Noirmoutiers	
17.	Paris	1841, 1 Jan.			1899, 26 June.
18.	Toulon	1841, 15 Aug.			
19.	Lyon	1842, 29 June.	38.	Metz	1834, 15 Aug.

ITALY.

1.	Rome	1838, 5 June.	5.	Villanova	1882, 26 Aug.
	(Provincial House).		6.	Portici	1885, 26 Oct.
2.	Rome	1840, 1 July.	7.	Rome	1895, 4 Nov.
3.	Capua	1860, 23 Sept.	8.	Chieti	1896, 26 April.
4.	Viterbo	1862, 25 April.			

No.	Date of the foundation.	No.	Date of the foundation.
1. Turin . . . 1843, 1 Nov. (Provincial House).		6. Reggio-Emilia 1857, 28 Nov.	
2. Imola . . . 1845, 20 Oct.		7. Forli . . . . 1859, 22 Jan.	
3. Bologna . . 1854, 16 July.		8. Monza . . . 1863, 8 April.	
4. Modena . . 1857, 4 Mar.		9. Faenza . . — 28 July.	
5. Genoa . . . — 25 Mar.		10. Turin . . . 1898, 3 May.	

1. Malta . . . 1858, 15 Oct. (Island of Malta, Provincial House).		3. Palermo . . 1878, 10 May.	
		4. Acireale . . 1887, 1 Dec.	
		5. Palermo . . 1898.	
2. Messina . . 1876, 28 Sept.		6. Catano . . —	

BELGIUM.

1. Namur . . 1840, 25 May. (Provincial House).
2. Mons . . . 1839, 8 Dec.

3. Louvain . . 1864, 8 Dec.
4. Evère . . . 1873, 2 Aug.

HOLLAND.

1. Leiderdorp 1860, 30 Mar. (Provincial House).

2. Harlem . . 1879, 20 Aug.
3. Velp . . . . 1892, 4 May.

GERMANY.

1. Munich . . 1840, 30 May. (Provincial House).
2. Mayence . 1854, 18 Jan.

3. Ettmannsdorf 1861, 15 July.

1. Munster . . 1850, 16 Sept. (Provincial House).
2. Charlottenburg 1858, 11 Feb.
3. Breslau . . 1859, 19 Nov.

4. Almelo (Holland) 1876, 28 Aug.
5. Reinickendorf 1887, 14 April.
6. Marxheim 1891, 29 Aug.
7. Beuthen . 1893, 15 Aug.

1. Cologne . . 1862, 21 Nov. (Provincial House).
2. Strasbourg (Alsace-Lorraine) . . 1837, 15 May.
3. Aix-la-Chapelle 1848, 21 Nov.

4. Trèves . . 1857, 15 Aug.
5. Mulhouse (Alsace) 1888, 7 Nov.
6. Coblentz . — 3 Dec.
7. Junkersdorf 1896, 9 June.

AUSTRIA AND HUNGARY.

No.	Date of the foundation.	No.	Date of the foundation.
1. Neudorf . .	1853, 8 Sept.	3. Gratz . . .	1858, 25 Dec.
(Provincial House).		4. Vienna . .	1867, 30 May.
2. Baumgartenberg		5. Harbach .	1890, 13 April.
	1856, 30 Nov.	6. Bu.la-Pest	1892, 31 July.

SWITZERLAND.

1. Altstœtten 1868, 16 April.

ENGLAND.

1. London . . 1864, 5 Aug.
(Provincial House).
2. London . . 1841, 25 Mar.
3. Glasgow (Scotland)
1851, 19 Mar.
4. Bristol . . . — 19 July.
5. Liverpool . 1858, 18 April.
6. Manchester 1867, 3 Feb.
7. Cardiff (Wales)
1872, 1 Nov.
8. Newcastle 1888, 27 Oct.
9. Ashford (Middlesex)
1899, 19 Mar.

IRELAND.

1. Limerick . 1848, 17 Mar.
(Provincial House).
2. Waterford 1858, 18 April.
3. New Ross. 1860, 16 May.
4. Belfast . . 1867, 15 Sept.
5. Cork . . . . 1870, 30 Mar.

SPAIN AND PORTUGAL.

1. Barcelona . 1880, 2 Oct.
2. Oporto . . 1881, 2 July.
3. Lisbon . . 1887, 4 Feb.

INDIA.

1. Bangalore 1854, 15 Aug.
2. Bellary . . 1865, 31 July.
3. Rangoon . 1866, 8 Feb.
4. Colombo (Ceylon)
1869, 25 April.
5. Mysore . . 1878, 8 Sept.
6. Kandy (Ceylon)
1888, June.

ALGERIA.

1. El-Biar . . 1843, 1 May.
(Provincial House).
2. Miserghin . 1851, 22 April.
3. Constantine 1855, 16 April.

EGYPT.

No.		Date of the foundation	No.		Date of the foundation
1.	Cairo	1846, 6 Jan.	5.	Asile Couvreux	1894, 10 Dec.
	(Provincial House).		6.	Hammana (Syria)	1893, 17 May.
2.	Cairo	1846, 6 Jan.			
3.	Port Said	1863, 19 April.			
4.	Suez	1865, 31 May.			

CANADA.

1. Montreal . 1844, 24 May.	4. Montreal . 1878, 14 Sept.
(Provincial House).	5. Halifax . . 1890, 13 June.
2. Montreal . 1870, 30 Mar.	6. St. John . 1893, 15 Aug.
3. St. Hubert — 3 May.	7. Loretto . . 1896.

UNITED STATES.

1. St. Louis . 1849, 29 Jan.
 (Provincial House).
2. New Orleans
 1859, 13 Mar.
3. Chicago . . — 20 May.
4. Memphis . 1875, 21 Nov.

5. Milwaukee 1877, 25 Dec.
6. Havana . . 1879, 8 Dec.
7. Normandy 1883, 26 Aug.
8. Kansas City 1887, 29 June.
9. Chicago . . — 23 Sept.
10. Peoria . . . 1891, 31 July.

1. Philadelphia (Provincial House) . . 1850, 15 May.
2. Baltimore 1864, 6 Aug.
3. West Philadelphia 1867, 15 Sept.
4. Washington 1883, 16 Aug.

5. Norristown 1886, 9 May.
6. Scranton . 1889, 25 Jan.
7. Reading . — 6 Mar.
8. Germantown 1892, 25 Mar.
9. Baltimore . — 29 Sept.

1. Carthage . 1892, 10 June.
 (Provincial House).
2. Louisville . 1843, 8 Sept.
3. Cincinnati 1857, 26 Feb.
4. Cincinnati 1863, 9 Mar.
5. Columbus . 1865, 8 May.

6. Louisville . 1866, 18 Aug.
7. Newport . — 1 May.
8. Cleveland . 1869, 24 July.
9. Indianapolis 1873, 19 Mar.
10. Detroit . . 1883, 23 Sept.

1. Brooklyn, New York
 1868, 8 May.
 (Provincial House).
2. New York 1857, 22 Sept.
3. Boston . . 1867, 1 May.
4. Mount Florence, Peekshill
 1867, 18 Oct.

5. Newark . . 1875, 24 May.
6. Troy . . . 1884, 20 June.
7. Albany . . 1887, 23 Jan.
8. Port of Spain (Trinidad)
 1890, Jan.
9. Springfield 1893, 1 Nov.

No.	Date of the foundation.	No.	Date of the foundation.
1. St. Paul	1868, 21 May.	4. Helena	1889, 11 Feb.
(Provincial House).		5. Seattle	1890, Aug.
2. Denver	1883, 30 Sept.	6. South Omaha	
3. Minneapolis	1888, 3 Nov.		1894, 8 April.

CHILI.

1. Santiago	1857, 22 Feb.	8. Santiago	1882, 15 June.
(Provincial House).		9. Santiago	1883, 5 Aug.
2. San Felipe	1855, 28 May.	10. Los Anjeles	1884, 7 Mar.
3. Valparaiso	1860, 29 Jan.	11. Conception	— 24 April.
4. Talca	1863, 24 Sept.	12. Chillan	— 20 June.
5. Santiago	1864, 17 April.	13. Cauquenes	1885, 20 June.
6. Curico	1881, 8 Feb.	14. Rancagna	1891, 25 Nov.
7. Quillota	— 5 Oct.		

La Serena 1861, 28 April. | Ovalle .. 1889, 2 Mar.

PERU.

1. Lima ... 1871, 14 Dec. | 2. Lima ... 1891, 12 April.
(Provincial House).

BOLIVIA.

3. La Paz .. 1892, 14 July. |

ECUADOR.

4. Quito ... 1871, 2 Aug. | 5. Cuenca .. 1892, 4 Oct.

COLUMBIA.

Bogota .. 1890, Mar. |

ARGENTINE REPUBLIC.

1. Buenos-Ayres 1885, 15 Oct. (Provincial House).	9. Buenos-Ayres 1890, 15 Jan.
2. Montevideo 1876, 3 Mar.	10. Rosario de Santa Fè 1892, 24 April.
3. Mendoza . 1886, 26 July.	11. Salta ... 1893, 3 Nov.
4. Cordova . 1889, 1 Jan.	12. Buenos-Ayres 1895, 13 Mar.
5. San-Luis . — 12 Feb.	
6. San-Juan . — 21 April.	13. Catamarca 1896, 12 June.
7. Tucuman . — 5 May.	14. Buenos-Ayres
8. Jujui ... — 30 May.	1898, 1 June.

BRAZIL.

| No. | Date of the foundation. | No. | Date of the foundation. |

15. Rio de Janeiro 1891, 31 July.
16. Bahia . . . 1892, 19 Oct.
17. Sao Paulo 1897, 2 May.

AUSTRALIA.

1. Melbourne 1863, 22 July. (Provincial House).
2. Oakleigh . 1883, 22 Dec.
3. South Melbourne 1893, 22 Jan.

NEW ZEALAND.

4. Christchurch 1886, 22 July.

TASMANIA.

5. Hobart . . 1893, 10 April.

TABLE OF CONTENTS.

	PAGE
Notice	7
Approbation from Rome of Mass proper to the Feast on 8th of February	11
Of the Office in General	13
Particular Observations	13
Calendar of Fixed Feasts	16

Movable Feasts—

Advent ...	32
Septuagesima ...	32
The Forty Hours	32
Ash Wednesday ...	33
Palm Sunday	34
The Three Days of Tenebræ	35
Easter Sunday, Notice for the Paschal Time ...	44
Feasts which fall during Paschal Time	45
Corpus Christi	46

Ceremonial of the Choir—

On Entering the Choir for the Office ...	47
Of the Sister who Officiates ...	48
First Chanter	50
Second Chanter, First Chorist ...	51
Second Chorist	52
Of those who ought to Supply for the Absent	52

K

Ceremonies of the Office—

	PAGE
Of the Order to be Observed when the Superior Officiates ...	57
Of the Order to be Observed when the Assistant Officiates ...	60
Of the Office of the Third Feasts	60
The Office of the Dead	61
Observations on the Office	62
Of the Sermons ...	66
Of Reverence and Tranquillity	66
On Entering and Leaving the Choir ...	66
The Times when the Office may be Advanced or Delayed ...	67
The Processions ...	68
The Ceremonies and Order which must be Observed when Holy Mass is Sung ...	69
Ceremonies for Low Mass	72
The Kiss of Peace	72
The Bells ...	73
Intentions for the Customary Prayers ...	75
Prayers said at the Canonical Visitation	77
Confirmation ...	79
Profession of Faith ...	80
Hours to which Matins may be Advanced for following Day ...	81

Ceremonial of the Last Sacraments ... 82

Holy Communion ...	82
Extreme Unction ...	87
Pious Reflections for Extreme Unction ...	87
Form of Conferring the Last Blessing and Plenary Indulgence ...	91
Recommendation of the Soul ...	93
The Agony ...	94
Prayers for the Agonizing ...	95
Three Devout and Profitable Prayers for the Agony ...	106

	PAGE
Of the Death ...	... 107
After the Death	... 108
Bells to be Rung at the Death ...	... 109
Directions for Laying out the Body	110
The Removal of the Body	... 111
The Burial	... 113
The Prayers and Suffrages for the Deceased Sisters	... 121
The Bells to be Rung for the Office of the Dead which is said for the Religious, and on the Anniversary of the Founders	... 124
When the Last Sacraments are Administered to the Penitents	... 124
The Decease of the Penitents	... 125
Benediction of the Blessed Sacrament	... 126
Extract from Bull of Paul V. ...	... 130
Privileges	... 133
Observation	... 135
Little Office of the Immaculate Conception	i
Convents of the Congregation of Our Lady of Charity of the Good Shepherd of Angers ...	x

RUBRICS.

1. The Religious of Our Lady of Charity of the Good Shepherd say for their Ordinary Office the Little Office of the Blessed Virgin, as it has been revised by the holy Council of Trent and Pope Urban VIII. Nevertheless they recite the Great Office, according to the Roman Breviary, on Christmas Day, the three last days of Holy Week, Easter Sunday, Pentecost, the Feast of the Sacred Heart of Jesus, the Sacred Heart of Mary, the Feast of Our Lady of Charity of the Good Shepherd, and of SS. Peter and Paul.

2. The Little Office of the Blessed Virgin, (which, however, does not oblige under pain of sin, as the Sacred Congregation of Bishops and Regulars has several times declared) takes the place of the Great Office for them; they say it in union with Holy Church, and with the intention of reciting it in her name, honoring, moreover, by the Commemorations, the mysteries and the Saints of which the Church celebrates the Feast.

3. Attention must be given to the following rules in order easily to find the Commemorations of Vespers and Lauds.

I. GENERAL RULE FOR THE COMMEMORATIONS.

The Commemorations are not transferred, that is, they are made on the same day on which they occur, or else entirely omitted, as will be explained farther on. Nevertheless, the Feasts of the Purification, the Annunciation and Saint Joseph, are transferred to the following Monday, when they fall on a privileged Sunday. When the Annunciation falls in Holy Week or Easter Week, it is put off to the Monday after the Sunday in Albis. When the Fast of St. Joseph falls in Holy Week, it is transferred to Wednesday after the Sunday in Albis. The Commemoration of the Holy Name of Jesus is taken on the 28th of January if Septuagesima Sunday falls on the second Sunday after Epiphany. Feasts of the rank of Double Major and the commemoration of Doctors, are transferred to the day market in the Ordo of the diocese if they fall on a privileged Sunday. The same rule is observed when a Feast of Double Major rite or the commemoration of a Doctor falls on an Octave Day, or a privileged Feria, or within the Octaves of Easter and Pentecost.

II. OF THE FEASTS.

The Feasts according to the Roman rite are divided into Double, Semi-double, and Simple Feasts.

1. The Double Feasts are subdivided into four classes, according to their greater or lesser degree of solemnity; doubles of the First Class, doubles of the Second Class, Doubles Major, Doubles Minor or Ordinary Doubles. On all Double Feasts the Anthems are doubled at Matins and Lauds, and at the First and Second Vespers, that is, the Anthem is said entirely, before and after the corresponding Psalm. But at Complin, Prime, Tierce and None, the first word or words of the Anthem are only said before the Psalms, the entire Anthem is said after the Psalms.

2. The Doubles of the First Class are; Easter with the three days preceding and two days following, Pentecost with the two days following, the Epiphany, Christmas, Corpus Christi, the Ascension, the Assumption, the Annunciation, the Immaculate Conception, St. Joseph, All Saints, the Nativity of St. John the Baptist, the Feast of SS. Peter and Paul, the titular Feast of the church, the Patron of the place, the Dedication of the church of each house, if it has been consecrated, the Feasts of the Sacred Heart of Jesus, the Sacred Heart of Mary, and the Feast of St. Augustin.

NOTE. — If several of these Feasts or their Octaves fall together, the commemoration of them shall be regulated after the order in which they are placed above.

3. In order to know the Doubles of the Second Class, Doubles Major, Ordinary Doubles, and Semi-doubles, the calendar must be consulted.

The greater number of the Doubles of the First Class, mentioned in No. 2, and some Doubles of the Second Class have Octaves, that is to say, they are celebrated during eight successive days. The six days that follow the Feast have the rite of Semi-double, the last day is Double. The Octaves of Easter and Pentecost are exceptions; the two first days are Doubles of the First Class. It must be observed that all Octaves cease from Ash Wednesday until the Sunday in Albis inclusively, and from the Vigil of Pentecost until Trinity Sunday. From December 17th until the Epiphany no Octaves can be kept, except those indicated in the Breviary.

As all Doubles and Semi-Doubles have First and Second Vespers, the Religious of the Good Shepherd may make commemoration of them at the First Vespers, which are said on the Eve, at Lauds of the day itself, and at Second Vespers, unless there should be one of the exceptions hereafter marked.

6. Simple Feasts are those which are designated under this title in the calendar, and those falling on a day that is Double or Semi-double, are indicated as Commemorations, for example, on Januar 14th, St. Felix is of simple rite. Simple Feasts, having no second Vespers, can only be commemorated at First Vespers and at the Lauds of the day itself, except on Doubles of the First Class, when no commemoration is made of a Simple Feast.

III. OF THE SUNDAYS.

Three sorts of Sundays are distinguished, privileged Sundays of the First Class, which are the First Sundays of Advent and Lent, Passion Sunday, Palm Sunday, Easter and Pentecost (of which the Sisters say the Office), Sunday in Albis and Trinity Sunday. Privileged Sundays of the Second Class, which are the 2nd, 3rd and 4th Sundays of Advent and Lent, Septuagesima, Sexagesima, and Quinquagesima Sundays. The others are called Ordinary Sundays. All Sundays (except Sunday in Albis, which is double, and Trinity Sunday, of which the Office is Double of Second Class) are of semi double rite, and consequently have First and Second Vespers. The First are those indicated for Saturday before these same Sundays.

IV. OF THE FERIAS, EMBER-DAYS AND VIGILS.

Two sorts of Ferias, or days of the week, are distinguished : ordinary Ferias, of which no commemoration is ever made, and Major Ferias of Advent and Lent, the Ember-days, and the Monday of the Rogation days, of which a commemoration is always made. Amongst these Major Ferias, four are Privileged : Ash Wednesday, Monday, Tuesday and Wednesday of Holy Week : (Maundy Thursday, Good Friday and Holy Saturday, are Doubles of the First Class). The Ferias of Advent and Lent have a Commemoration at Lauds and Vespers of the Day.

The Spring Ember-days, which are kept in the first week of Lent, and those of Winter in the third week of Advent come under the rule of Major Ferias of Advent and Lent. The Summer Ember-days are kept during the privileged Octave of Pentecost, and count as a day of the Octave. The Ember-days of September and Monday of the Rogation days have a commemoration only at Lauds.

3. The Vigils or Eves of certain Feasts may be considered as Major Ferias, but they have commemoration only at Lauds of the day, and this commemoration is omitted on a double of the First Class. An exception, however, is made for the Vigils of Christmas, Epiphany and Pentecost. The Vigils of Christmas and Epiphany are the only ones which are made on a Sunday, if they fall on that day. Other Vigils which occur on Sunday are anticipated on the preceding Saturday.

V. OF THE MANNER OF MAKING THE COMMEMORATIONS.

The Commemorations are only made at Vespers and Lauds. They are made immediately after the prayer of Vespers or Lauds of the Office of the Blessed Virgin, before the Anthem "Sancti Dei omnes", or "Ecce Dominus veniet".

2. Every commemoration is composed of an Anthem, a corresponding V. and R. and a Prayer. The Anthem, V. R., and Prayer are taken from the Proper of the Season, or of the Saints, or else from the Common. (What is wanting in the Proper of the Saints is always taken from the Common).

3. As the first and last prayer only are terminated, and as, on the other hand, the Commemorations thus added to the Office of the Blessed Virgin, are placed between the first prayer of Vespers and Lauds and the General Commemoration of the Saints: "Sancti Dei omnes," or "Ecce Dominus veniet," it follows that the prayers of the Commemorations are said without conclusion. In reciting the Office the indication of the conclusion must be suppressed, which has only been marked in case, that for some reason or other, these prayers should be said apart from the Office.

NOTE.—On Doubles of First and Second Class, and during the Octaves of Easter Pentecost, Epiphany, Corpus Christi and Christmas, the General Commemoration of the Saints is omitted, and only those marked for the Feast or the Octave are made. In this case the prayer of the Feast, or the last prayer of the day should have the great conclusion.

4. If two commemorations occur together of which the Anthems or versicles are the same, for example: two Confessors not Bishops, for the second commemoration at First Vespers, the Anthem or V. of Lauds is taken, and at Lauds the Anthem or V. of the First Vespers. The V. *Laetamini*, which is said after the Sancti Dei of the Ordinary Office, is also found at the Common of the Martyrs, and must be replaced by *Exultabunt Sancti in gloria*. When a third V. and R. are needed the following is taken for the Martyrs:

V. Exultent justi in conspectu Dei—
R. Et delectentur in laetitia. (Breviary Nov. 4th.)

For Confessors who are Bishops is taken:
V. Elegit eum Dominus sacerdotem sibi—
R. Ad sacrificandum et hostiam laudis. (January 14th.)

For Confessors, not Bishops:
V. Os justi mediatabitur sapientiam—
R. Et lingua ejus loquetur judicium—

For Virgins:
V. Elegit eam Deus et praelegit eam :
R. In tabernaculo suo habitare facit eam.

VI. OF THE ORDER WHICH MUST BE FOLLOWED WHEN SEVERAL COMMEMORATIONS COME TOGETHER.

For the Commemorations the order of solemnity is followed, that is, the commemoration of the Feast of a superior rite always goes before that of an inferior rite. The following is the order of solemnity :

1. Doubles of First Class.
2. Doubles of Second Class.
3. Octave Days.
4. Privileged Sundays (Dimanches Majeurs).
5. Doubles Major.
6. Ordinary Doubles.
7. Ordinary Sundays.
8. Days within the Octave of Corpus Christi.
9. Semi-doubles.
10. The six days in a non-privileged Octave.
11. Major Ferias and Ordinary Vigils.
12. The Simple Feasts.

First Exception: The Commemoration of the Privileged Sundays of the First Class passes before all others at Lauds, as also that of Privileged Major Ferias, and the Vigils of Christmas, Pentecost and Epiphany. The Commemoration of the First Vespers of these Sundays, that is, of the Saturday which precedes them, as well as that of the Second Vespers of these same Sundays, is taken before semi-doubles, and even of minor Doubles if these latter fall on the same day, for in this case, the Church makes the Office of the Sunday, and only a commemoration is made of the Double Minor which, according to the decision of the Sacred Congregation of Rites is then simplified.

Second Exception: The Commemoration of Privileged Sundays of the Second Class, is taken before all Feasts which are not First Class, at Lauds only, for at Vespers a Double of the Second Class would have precedence.

Third Exception: The Commemoration of the Privileged Octaves of Easter, Pentecost and Epiphany, is made before all others; if, however, the titular feast of the church, the holy patron of the place, and the Dedication of the church, falls on one of the six days in the Octave of the Epiphany, its commemoration is placed before that of the Octave; in the same manner if the Holy Name of Jesus falls on the 14th of January, the Second Vespers of the Octave of the Epiphany, commemoration would first be made of the Holy Name of Jesus, then the Second Vespers of the Epiphany, afterwards of St. Hilary and the Sunday.

Fourth Exception: The Commemoration of the Vigil of Christmas, when it falls on Sunday, precedes the Commemoration of the Sunday.

When two Feasts are of the same rite, for example, two Doubles Major, the Feast of the greater dignity is made first, and if the dignity be the same, the first Vespers of the Feast of the next day is made before the Second Vespers of the Feast of the day.

The following is the order of dignity: 1. The Feasts of Our Lord. 2. Feasts of the Blessed Virgin. 3. Feasts of the Holy Angels. 4. The Feast of St. John the Baptist. 5. The Feasts of St. Joseph. 6. The Feasts of the Apostles and Evangelists.

The Feasts of the other Saints, without distinction, are placed in the same rank.

But when one of two Feasts is primary or principal, and the other secondary, no notice is taken of the dignity, the primary Feast goes first; the rule just stated applies only in the case where the two Feasts are equal, that is to say, if both are primary or both secondary.

NOTE.—All Feasts are considered secondary, which may be regarded as the appendage of another Feast; for example, the Patronage of St. Joseph is a secondary Feast, because St. Joseph already had his Feast on March 19th; the same of the Feasts of the Passion which are celebrated on the Fridays of Lent; they are secondary Feasts. If then, the Feast of St. Benedict, of Double Major rite, falls on a Friday in Lent, the commemoration of St. Benedict goes before that of Our Lord, because St. Benedict has but one Feast during the year, while Our Lord has several. The Feast of St. Benedict is therefore called primary, and that of Our Lord is but secondary.

As the Octaves are only a continuation of the Feast during eight days, at Lauds the commemoration is made of the Lauds of the Feast, and at Vespers the commemoration of the Second Vespers of the Feast. Nevertheless, at the Vespers of the seventh day, commemoration is made of the First Vespers of the Feast, because the Octave, being Double, has its First and Second Vespers.

When two or more Octaves come together, commemoration is first made of that of the highest rite, that is, the Octave of a Double of the First Class goes before that of a Double of the Second Class.

VII. FEASTS OF THE FIRST AND SECOND CLASS WHICH EXCLUDE CERTAIN COMMEMORATIONS.

At the First Vespers of a Double of the First Class the commemoration of the Second Vespers of a Double Major or Minor, of a non-privileged Sunday, of a Semi-double or of a day in the Octave, is omitted. But a commemoration is made of the second Vespers of a Feast of the First and Second Class, and of a Privileged Feria of Advent and Lent. A commemoration is also made of the First Vespers of any Sunday whatever, of an Octave Day (the Octave Day, or eighth day after a solemn Feast, must not be confounded with the six days that follow the Feast and are called days within the Octave), of any Feast whatever, and of a privileged Feria. At Lauds of a Double of the First Class a Commemoration is made of any Sunday whatever, of an Octave Day, and of a privileged Feria.

At the Second Vespers of a Double of the First Class the commemoration of the First Vespers of a Simple Feast is omitted, but a commemoration is made of the First Vespers of any Sunday whatever, of any Double or Semi-double whatever, even though simplified, of a day in the Octave (if the Office of the Day in the Octave is made the following day, according to the Breviary) and of Major Ferias.

At the First Vespers of a Double of the Second Class the Commemoration of the Second Vespers is omitted:
 1. Of a Semi-double Feast,
 2. Of a non-privileged Sunday,
 3. Of a day within the Octave.

But a commemoration is made of the Second Vespers:
 1. Of any double whatever,
 2. Of a privileged Sunday.

A commemoration is also made of the First Vespers:
 1. Of any Double whatever,
 2. Of any Sunday whatever,
 3. Of a Semi-double.
 4. Of a Major Feria.

At the Lauds of a Double of the Second Class all the commemorations which occur are made, ever of a Simple Feast, the commemoration of a day in the Octave alone is suppressed.

At the Second Vespers of a Double of the Second Class the commemoration of a day in the Octave is omitted, unless the Office of the same is made the following day in the Breviary. A commemoration is made of any Sunday whatever, of any Double or semi-double whatever, and also of a Simple Feast and of any Major Feria whatever.

The other Feasts which are not Doubles of the First or Second Class admit all the commemorations which occur.

www.ingramcontent.com/pod-product-compliance
Lightning Source LLC
Chambersburg PA
CBHW031454160426
43195CB00010BB/971